Professionalism *in* **FLIP FLOPS**

By Ryan Kulp

Professionalism in Flip Flops
Copyright © 2012 by Ryan Kulp

ISBN: 978-0-9884924-0-0

Printed in the United States of America

"Flip Flops Are the Scourge of Professional Workplaces Everywhere"
–Jen Doll, The Village Voice

Contents

Chapter 1 | Question and Answer of Origin

*"I think I did pretty well, considering I started out
with nothing but a bunch of blank paper."*
–Steve Martin

I've spent the past two years at many a coffee shop outlining ideas for this book. I used whatever I could get my hands on, from Moleskine notebooks to digital memo pads on my BlackBerry or iPhone. Since graduating college, it's become increasingly important that I keep my mind occupied with thoughts other than vague 1980s sitcom references.

In this book I've done my best to validate points with research and deductive reasoning—stuff I've pulled from surveying, statistics, and plenty of credential-loaded pinky-out type individuals. There is also banter, making it fun to read. So no, this is not a typical piece of non-fiction business literature.

While sales would be incredibly helpful for my quest to pursue new projects, my purpose in writing this book is to share information. I figured during my junior year of college that all the time, money, and effort I've spent reading books, listening to professors, and observing life could be abridged in an entertaining but meaningful sort of memoir. This book is that idea, come to fruition.

1

More than anything, this book is a recollection of my pint-sized life. You might find my life to be boring and pathetic—that's OK. I've always worn my heart on my sleeve and I think transparency is one of the best ways to achieve understanding.

Therefore, this book touches on more than just business acumen and entrepreneurship in the 21st century. I offer full disclosure of all aspects to my life, ranging from my spiritual to mental and physical convictions.

Being as concise and direct as I know how to be, I break down false faculties supporting what I call the Executive Facade. Through reading, you will find what variables are most often attributed to professional, winning mentalities along with the profitable change they inevitably harvest. Rather than reinvent the wheel, this book intends to hold dear the most efficient business practicums, while rejecting those steeping in tradition or sought-after in university lecture halls.

If there is only one thing unique about this book, it is that a non-author wrote it. Like when Woody Boyd in Cheers runs for office not as a politician but as a true "public servant." (See what I did there?)

Moreover, I write this as a non-scholar. Disclaimer: I'm barely out of college, and should probably be looking for a job instead of writing about them.

But this is the 21st century. I am of the Y Generation. We are in the Information Age. And information is power.

So before you continue, please connect with me on LinkedIn. Shoot over your questions (or nasty comments) as you read and let's make this an interactive discussion. Gone are the days of linear intelligence and rote learning. Also, visit the supplementary reading links provided throughout the book. They will guide you to even more goodies and resources that I couldn't fit on a page or couldn't afford a publisher to print.

Still, the question keeps nagging at my pant leg: why should you read this book?

Because you have a knack for getting busted at the office, or can't stand the age-old traditions that haunt America's workplaces. When you got passed up for a promotion, you stood idly by and called it "life." When a superior gives you unwarranted feedback, you apologize and promise to not let it happen again.

3

You don't live to work, you simply work to live. Your job doesn't define you, because it knows nothing about you. You have skills and talents that no one at your workplace would understand or discover; after all, you're not challenged enough.

Henceforth, you want a fresh perspective on business. You also have 3 hours of free time.

Welcome.

Chapter 2 | Behind the Pseudo-Intellectualism

"You know Ryan, I won't be fooled by your weird
sense of pseudo-intellectualism."
—High school guidance counselor

A quick life story:

I was born and raised in the burbs of Atlanta,
Georgia. My father worked for a tower company and
my mother an accounting department. As the first-
born I was given a lot of attention. Going to the
grocery store with my dad meant going home with
all the Kool-Aid 6-packs I could hold in my short,
chubby arms. I'm talking multiple flavors. We lived a
middle class life in a four-bedroom house with a
small, unfinished basement. My dad turned this into
my playroom, with thin carpet on the floor and
cement walls painted navy blue for a less *"puts the
lotion in the basket"* kind of aesthetic.

Just after my third birthday I received a belated
present: a baby brother. His name was Kevin and he
was all the rage at the Kulp crib. He even got his
own. Needless to say, the Kool-Aid runs came to a
halt and our carts were soon filled with diapers and
baby food. I really enjoyed leftovers from those

small glass treats and often got face-slapped for partaking in my brother's livelihood. Or lifeblood. Two friends consumed my 4-year-old life and both lived in the same house at different times. Let's call the first one Katie, because for the life of me I cannot remember why I rode in her miniature Barbie car. Remember those pink blobs of inefficient plastic? It went 6 miles per hour and the battery ran dry after a few runs around the cul-de-sac. We cruised like cruisers do, watching people as they watched us. When Katie moved out, her replacement (aka my new best friend) was Wesley. He had an entire kitchen set of Ronald McDonald cook-at-home appliances that simulated actual food processing machines at McDonald's. For example, a bread slicer turned a small bread slice into French fries. Just like the real thing.

For my fifth birthday we got a new house, just a few miles away and in a more developed area. Later I found out this meant more white people lived there. I began kindergarten and watched as my brother learned to walk. My hygiene must have been off the chain because my mom required that I brushed my teeth after every meal at school. Thankfully my classroom was lavished with sinks and those small, centimeter length light brown tiles.

My first grade teacher, Mrs. Benner, was awesome. An entire corner of her classroom was called "The Reading Corral" and was fancied up much like a bad western movie set. Instead of chairs it was furnished with pillows and a nasty noose rope that gave one splinters just looking at it. It was also in this period of life I realized my IQ was above average. My mom took me to the public library every week where I picked out a score of Goosebumps and other R.L. Stein masterpieces. There was a 30 minute required reading period in my daily schedule, but it came like no chore. I loved to read.

Another dimension of my life that existed from age 5 to 16 was my involvement with recreational sports. I tried t-ball, little league, tennis, wrestling and track. I wasn't good at any of them.

Moving on to middle school—actually, let's go back for a moment. Days before my fifth grade graduation, the entire grade level got to walk through the hallways of our school to be respected by the underclassmen. Everyone in grades K-4 had to stand outside their homerooms and watch as we boasted our double-digit age group amongst other petty and inevitable achievements. Eight standardized tests further along than they, we were of a superior race: alumni. Playing in the background was the song *As We Go On*, a sentimental pop tune sung by one-hit-wonder Vitamin C. I mention this because my neighbor, let's call her Jane, threw up all over the floor while sobbing uncontrollably.

In sixth grade I picked up a new hobby. I loved to skate and I hung out with other skater kids who were significantly older than me. I'm talking driver's permits. I even had a shirt describing my new persona with unique precision: "I'm not bad, I'm just not good." And so the charade lasted a couple years. We grinded, jumped, spun, and even made films to mail in for sponsorships (pre-YouTube, people). Needless to say we received none, most likely because my heavy breathing was picked up by budget camcorder's microphone. Well, that and also the fact that we sucked.

I got into a bit of trouble during my early teen era with detentions, write-ups, and even suspension from school for selling firecrackers. I knew from the beginning it was dumb to retail explosives, but the profit margins were out of control.

My first girlfriend, a blonde, was a catalyst: the beginning of the end of my teenage angst. She had me over all the time to watch James Bond movies (her stepdad had the entire collection). We went on neighborhood walks, a slight progression from the Barbie car rides, and we kissed for several seconds at a time. It was glorious. By the end of eighth grade my skater ties had been broken, and the blonde moved away to Alabama where her dumb country accent proved a better fit. Heartbroken, I was. Soon however I became preoccupied with other things, like putting forth a James Bond effort into the guitar I had gotten for my 13th birthday. Wooing the television and other objects in my room became an obsession. I was serenating toy trains and my waist tall cd tower long before thin glass windows of a girl next door's two-story house. Not to mention it was cheap, too. While my other friends were busy getting dropped off at adolescent paradise (the mall) or Wal-Mart to walk around and spend $6 in the food court on subpar Chinese, I was alone in my bedroom learning *Kum Ba Yah*.

High school rolled around and I got involved in church. I was saved, and still am, by the grace of God. To serve Him I played guitar and sang on Sundays for the next four years, with my title being worship leader and my employers the youth and adult praise bands. I also met someone. Everyone in school knew her as the genius with a rhyming name. I just called her "hey, you." We became biffles (BFF) and began strumming our guitars in sync on the weekends. We swapped tunes and learned a lot about friendship.

Outside of my church involvement, I started a rock band. We even had a screamer for an added, deafening touch. A couple new names and four lineup changes later, we were solid. Our band was called "The Last Great Bridge Jumper." Like I said, solid.

While none of the rock star aspirations panned out for us, I did gain a lot of great experience as a performer, and dozens of stories I'll remember till my death. Like one time where we kicked out a band member on the way to a show which was over a hundred miles away. He got out of the car and then convinced the other half of the band in our second vehicle to quit with him. So the screamer and I went to the gig alone and played a 45-minute acoustic set, mixing originals with tribute covers. There were 80 people sitting on the venue's floor Indian-style, chanting and singing beautifully along to the music. Lighters and cell phones alike were lit up and waved side to side. The evening was magical, and the band got back together the next morning. That may have been the best gig I've ever played, and currently my number of live performances exceeds three hundred.

Since hindsight is 20/20, it wasn't until *after* I chose not to apply to colleges that I realized the music thing was too premature to yield success. I watched as all my friends went to community colleges, state universities, and, more sadly, as my female friend began her freshman year at a school up north. At this point I had a cool new job making gold teeth, also known as grills, which are worn in the mouths of people with terribly tacky taste. But the money was good and rent was free, as I was housesitting for a neighbor and eating all the perishables in their pantry. I skipped around the country several times and even recorded my own solo album. The style was acoustic rock, much different than my previous endeavor, and I actually sold a few copies.

I began college—or "uni" for ye Canadians—a semester later than my high school friends. With a newfound ambition to play corporate games and jump through the hoops of a four-year formality, I went 3 semesters straight with a 4.1 GPA. My high school finish was 2.75. During college, I took advantage of every opportunity and built an extensive resume composed of marketing, management, leadership, tech, and startup experience. I sacrificed a lot. One time while setting up a huge sound system at 3am for a corporate event, my roommates called and said our house had just been invaded. The perpetrator took my Xbox and some community items like our pink bb gun. This is what happens when you stay late at work and don't have time for your family. Err, roommates.

It is the culmination of my sacrifices, learned skills, sit-ins on boring lectures, and general lack of ever finding contentment, that compelled me to write this book. I also think it might impress an employer to hand over a copy of my book (in lieu of my résumé) if I ever score a real interview.

Too bad I'm not looking for a real job.

Chapter 3 | God?

*Christianity, if false, is of no importance, and if true,
of infinite importance. The only thing it cannot be is
moderately important.*
−C. S. Lewis

Somewhere along the thread lines of universal truths
and understanding there is a moral spine that holds
people together. The geographic exceptions are
those tribes in Africa who mutilate women's
genitals. They are not people; they are monsters.

This backbone of secular commandments is rarely
debated, but recently it changed its name to what
hipsters and crunchy granola kids call "Human
Rights." These Rights propose that we should not
steal, kill or cheat. And outside of those
aforementioned African tribes, we have 180+
nations whose laws enforce consequences for
breaking those ideals.

It only makes sense, then, that these same
guidelines of conduct might have come from
somewhere other than a single human's opinion.
Because while nations and peoples weren't
connected until the middle of this past millennium,
ancient writings and documents bear similar
reasoning from thousands of years prior.

Doesn't 2+2 = 4 in outer space as it does in Melbourne or the North Pole?

As it relates to professionalism and business, we see a pattern at college campuses today offering courses on "business ethics." These courses, often taught by academics with little or no experience in the private sector, teach us the do's and don'ts in the real world of business. We are advised against insider trading (cheating), bad environmental policies (killing/devastation), and hostile takeovers of smaller companies (stealing). Do you see the trend?

Because of this, I am compelled to mention the notion of God, or an intelligent designer who might have created these practicums for us to live by. And if you don't want anything to do with universal fairness, equality, and mutual understanding between different groups of people, feel free to skip the rest of this chapter. You'll only be missing out on psychological benefits that can increase your profits and decrease your stress.

First point: Karma. This is the secular translation of God's golden rule: treat your neighbors like you want to be treated. We prance around life doing some good while silently hoping it returns to us two-fold. And when someone else does wrong we are quick to bring up Karma and how "he'll get his." But what we're really saying here is we value the Golden Rule; we want to be treated with respect and share good fortune for returning that courtesy to others. So why do we call it Karma?

Second point: consequences. Wherever we live on this earth, we are most likely familiar with our local government's standards and procedures for a citizen who breaks the rules. Specifically, we know that lying, cheating, stealing and killing can earn us years in a jail cell or even death by lethal force. So, we watch as others make mistakes, then, as they're publicly humiliated, we let their remembrance serve as reminders and examples that we don't make the same choices. But this magnitude of consequence is just the tip of the iceberg because it is temporary. What if we could see the eternal consequence of someone's mistakes? What if there was a place that humans' spirits dwell following death? What if there were two places, one that was filled with happiness and the other with destruction and hopelessness? Christians call those places Heaven and Hell. What if we could check a database of dead people that documents who went where? Or who goes where, pending your stance on pre-destination? Would that compel us to look back at their lives and see what they did right (or wrong)? I think it would.

Nobel Prize winner Albert Camus once famously said, "I would rather live my life as if there is a god and die to find out there isn't, than live my life as if there isn't and die to find out there is." This was obviously a conscience decision made by Camus to behave in certain ways and place value on some convictions over others. And, like most decisions, there is always risk involved. Any gambler will tell you "with great risk comes great reward," the mantra that motivates them to continue gambling. So why don't we clinch the remark of a brilliant, world-renowned author and philosopher? Is it because there is a small chance that eternal consequences don't exist? Is that a risk worth taking?

To examine further, let's compare how we usually debate risks of chance in our lives. Humans are funny creatures so it's worth taking a step back to look at our cross-sectional illogical nature. For example, the odds of us being killed in an airplane accident are 1 in 354,319. Yet, millions of people every year refuse to fly and instead resort to long, dangerous road trips or simply refrain from traveling at all. On the flip side, our odds of being killed in an auto accident are 77 to 1, and only 85% of Americans wear their seatbelts.

One thing separating humans from animals is emotion. We can feel real pain just by involving ourselves in someone else's. Deep stuff. And, as a result, our logic (deriving from somewhere, see first paragraph) is constantly flawed by clouded judgment (see above). So it only makes sense that our ability to assess a situation and its risk of consequence will not necessarily reflect logical behavior. Meaning, when considering the existence of God, shouldn't we admit our superstitions and follow the numbers?

Among the most debated topics in our modern day society is the existence of God.

Regardless of evidence or proof from either side, the mere interest of 6 billion humans makes it sufficient to say that we are a curious people who want answers about things bigger than ourselves. Why do we breathe oxygen? Why do we recreate? What happens after we die?

So I challenge you to embrace the words of Albert Camus and live like there might be a God—a god who will judge your life's choices and make decisions accordingly about your eternal spirit. Whether this means Heaven or Hell is up to you. Whether this means a proverbial pat on the back or a "try again next time" is up to you. And, whatever it means to "live like there is a God," is up to you. Just do it.

Chapter 4 | Terrible Bosses

"Management is doing things right; leadership is doing the right thing."
–Peter F. Drucker

For the purpose of this lively discussion on the perils of bad management, I have split into groups the different boss personalities I've encountered in my shrimp-sized career. Don't let my age dissuade you; while being just 22 years old may not yield in-depth experience, I assure you the breadth is quite adequate. In fact, since being legally able to work, I've reported to 15 different bosses in several industries. And yet one thing perturbs me...somehow the same patterns of management styles have been recycled over and over again.

I dabble in several types of work now, from freelance marketing to medical lab rat and economics experiments. In college I was the president of my university's programming board, a student brand manager for Red Bull, and a campus rep for Microsoft. I also started 2 profitable businesses during that time and networked the crap out of Atlanta, GA. I competed nationally in entrepreneurship competitions and held meetings with millionaires, celebrities, and philanthropists. I received numerous spots in publications for my music, scholastic, and business achievements. The resume keeps growing every day and sometimes I wake up late at night from a dream with the pulsing urge to tweak a word on my CV. But more importantly, I'm expanding my mind's horizon and finding stimulation in a dead society.

Across all my diverse experiences there is one constant: interaction with people. I think I've done a pretty good job faking it until I make it. Tim Roth says in the television drama *Lie to Me* that "Survival of the fittest is not about being fit, but being able to adapt." I couldn't agree more.

When I think about what it means to be a "boss," I cloud my judgment with conflicting management ideals. I tell myself some methods work better with certain people. That my Nazi boss at Lowe's Home Improvement could never have gotten away with his antics at a corporate office. But then I'm forced to reject that sentiment because it's simply not true.

We humans allow ourselves to be treated in peculiar ways. But if you mess with an animal, they'll fight to the death trying to tear you apart. Does that taste good in your mouth? And when a superior turns freak-psycho, we allow them to stomp all over us. So we must train the boss. As George Costanza from *Seinfeld* says, we must "get some hand." We must demand obedience from our superiors or we'll continue to hate this thing called life.

There are various boss-training methods, but all of them point to the same basic methodology. Ever hear the phrase, "Give a man an inch and he'll take a mile?" Inherent in those words is the infrastructure required to train your boss. As you naturally and inevitably gain trust, credibility, and stature at your place of employment, you will be given inches and centimeters of respect in reciprocity.

Most employees yell "Yippee!" and keep doing their job, completely stoked that they've been given a shred of recognition. How truly little they expect from this overbearing individual and organization they've given literally years of their lives too—let alone their sanity. Never mind the full cup they're due, the boss is just doing what he can! They surmise. Want to know a little secret? You *can* be different. You *can* do better. You can choose to take miles (or feet, or yards) and train the boss. That wild animal you call "sir" can no longer keep you jumping through hoops in the circus ring.

But we have to understand the boss before we can train them. The art of boss-hood requires two pillars of comprehension. It is only after we grasp these nuggets of understanding that we can begin to train the boss.

1 | We have to understand what they "do"
2 | We have to understand their character
3 | We have to understand the Boss-Employee Paradox

What Our Boss "Does"
A boss role usually separates itself from a subordinate's role by the difference between tactical and strategic work. Tactical operations are where real work gets *done*. A cellphone is manufactured, shipped and placed on a shelf. Strategic work is the planning and rationalization of the tactical work. Strategic work usually consists of asking and answering questions, such as *who* manufactures the product, *how* will it be shipped, and *where* on a shelf it will be placed.

With the exception of so-called middle management (you know, that group of people who got fired in 2008), most bosses have strategic duties while their subordinates have tactical duties. Neither is necessarily superior in and of itself, but it takes a different skillset to competently perform at either. We serfs often dream of being "The Boss" but do so by simply imagining ourselves doing the same stuff for more money. That, or we imagine doing "easier work" for more money. You might have heard a friend say, "All he does is sit there while we do all the work." A friend might have heard you say it, too.

Let's look further into tactical vs. strategic work by examining a few different departments of the made-up corporation fondly referred to as Acme Inc. Acme designs, produces, and sells products. It innovates its products regularly. It's building a brand so consumers can effectively differentiate. Acme keeps all of its own books and has a support team for end-users to contact if there's a problem with a product. In case you can't tell, Acme is a very typical corporation.

There's vertical integration, a bit of outsourcing, and just enough infrastructure to hold everything together. Some departments at Acme include Accounting, Marketing, Sales, Human Resources, Production, Research and Development, and Customer Service. Now let's see how tactical vs. strategic work is delegated in each.

Accounting / Finance

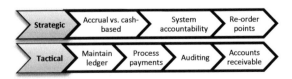

22

Marketing

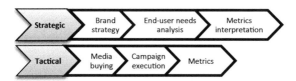

Sales

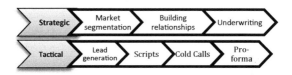

Human Resources

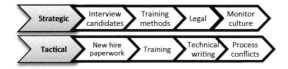

Production / Manufacturing

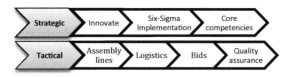

Research and Development

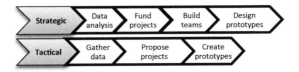

Customer Service

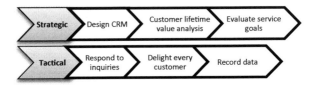

Do you see the translation of strategic responsibilities to tactical execution? This is what your boss "does."

Character – Not a Prerequisite

Next, let's try to understand the principles of life to which your boss subscribes. Is he religious? Does he watch a lot of reality TV? Is there a wife in his life, or a second, or a third? All of these factors are significant when observing behavior patterns. A religious person may put great emphasis on commitments. The TV-lover might romanticize fantasies and live vicariously through other people. An unmarried boss might be selfish or bitter.

While the above connotations are general and not always true, my point is that some aspects of our life come with (or without) a lot of other baggage. For all intents and purposes, that baggage is a set of behavioral patterns that we can often times attribute to a person's lifestyle.

We all have different circles of friends and occasionally when the timing is right we get introduced to friends of our friends. We all share the title "mutual friends" and sometimes it's awkward to spend time with a mutual friend. Why is this exactly? Basically, one of you knows everyone equally while everyone else is only comfortable with half the group. Typical dilemma of our so-called developed world of hyper-connectivity, right?!

Perhaps I'm alone on this, but I usually pass judgment on mutual friends after I'm alone again with my friend that introduced us. I'll say, "She seems weird" or "He's really weird," or something much nastier than that. Usually I get a response like, "You don't know what they've been through" or "Well she didn't tell you about _____." Of course, being the understanding and tolerant fellow I am, I silently take back my comments and give the mutual friend another chance to make a good impression on me. I do it because my main friend (the one who introduced us) has good judgment and it's easy to take their word for it.

When it comes to your boss, you have to remember that he was selected by someone who is now probably *his* boss. He was selected by that person or group for a bunch of reasons, and with any luck some of them are good ones. So before you pass judgment, you've got to acknowledge that this bozo did not come into his position with a dictatorial mentality. Rather, he seemed like a team player. And if you respect your boss' boss, you've got to give your boss another chance.

When you get to know your boss on a personal level, things usually begin to change immediately. The added effort it takes in the office to accomplish a personal rapport can be tricky, which is why I won't even try to coach you on it. Every company has a culture, a voice, and a generally accepted style of fraternization between employees. Ask your HR rep or someone at the water cooler how to better build a personal relationship with your boss. But whatever it takes, just do it.

The Boss-Employee Paradox
I'll keep it simple. Reminding yourself of this on a daily basis might help deter insanity. Whether you're

the queen or a pawn, there is a two-pronged universal truth to people management.

1 | A boss' idea of hard work is to push employees as far as possible without them quitting.
2 | An employee's idea of hard work is to perform as little as possible without getting fired.

Below are a few types of boss personalities I've worked with most in my snack-sized career. I'd like to think there is something here for everyone, so keep reading until one of the profiles "sticks." Then see what you can do about it.

The Delegator
I first discovered this boss profile in 2011 when I received 20+ emails on my way home from work. Upon checking them, I found each message was a mundane task assigned to me by a co-worker. At the time we used a project management tool called Basecamp, which allows large groups to collaborate on projects by assigning to-do lists to each other. It also increases accountability since everyone can see each other's workload. The downside, however, is that you can get 20+ emails on the way home from work.

I figured the flood of messages might just be the nature of the program, but ironically Jason Fried (creator of Basecamp) says in his book *Rework* that "the delegator is dead-weight."

My next action was to log in and browse my apparent to-do's. I commented on many of them with suggestions, only to be matched Devil's Advocate style against my every attempt to make progress.

Regardless of the software tools we use in the workplace, we are constantly "checking off" completed assignments. The difference, however, is what happens after an assignment is complete. Naturally it should be reviewed for errors and then pushed to the next team for further development. But the delegator simply assigns new tasks: new tactical behaviors.

With a delegator boss, you don't know whether a budget decision needs to be recanted or a sales strategy needs further revision. Nothing actually gets done. And while the delegator's intentions may be to create clear goals, they ultimately end up convincing employees that they don't have any real power at the company. How does that taste during the drive home? Can't it get any better than this?

The Micro-Manager

This person gets confused with the delegator because they indulge in similar wrongdoings. To differentiate, you can recognize the micro-manager by other giveaway behaviors and general temperance issues. For example, if you're constantly being asked, "Hey Bill, what are you working on?" then you probably have a micro-manager. In more intimate work environments it doesn't have to be as explicit; even a simple glance at your computer screen by a superior who has no business looking at your screen is sufficient evidence that you have a micro-manager.

Regarding temperance, a micro-manager is most often revealed when they designate trivial time intervals between status updates, i.e. the "mid-week" status report. Or even by sending reminder emails after not receiving a form of correspondence within 30 minutes of lunch hour being over. If you have the guts (and you should), it can actually be entertaining to watch them squirm in their chair and create countless excuses to elicit information from you, the actual producer.

For this boss type, I recommend a gradual distancing between your workflow and how privy your boss is to your progress. It will pay off in the long run when you can leave early on Friday without the worry of a stern look Monday morning.

The WTF

Perhaps the most loathed boss in all history of bosses. The bane of office life existence, if I may be so bold. This boss earned their title, position, and wages on unwarranted terms—nepotism, an overly political in-house promotional hiring campaign, or by the word everyone uses: connections.

We walk on a thin line with this one. I admit to receiving some jobs due to somewhat preferential treatment, however I also made sure to out-perform my peers while working them. Could Bill Gates give his son a great job in the dynasty? Of course! But would he also be quick to demote if Gates Jr. wasn't living up to the family standard? Absolutely.

Most companies, unfortunately, don't follow the same logic and don't have any moral compass. We now hear the saying "It's who you know" much more often than its second cousin, twice removed, "It's what you know." What a shame. But it isn't your job to fix this. You just need to recognize it.

If your boss is a snotty WTF type, remember to stay calm. Some day they will explode on you with unwarranted reasoning. If you play your cards right, you may just get them exterminated. I did it once myself, but my lawyers (my conscience) won't let me detail it in this book.

Head Herder
Suppose the owner of a dope-selling drug ring has a monthly sales quota. He can't spill this number to his subordinates. It will only result in one of two things and both are bad for the company: a) they exceed the goal and want raises, bonuses and perks, or b) they'll fear the daunting nature of their sudden, apparent incompetence. Since most people work just hard enough not to get fired, it's really difficult to assume the employees will practice collectivism or show any interest at all in the well-being of their employer.

Since complaint departments and ethics hotlines don't work very well in the dope world, the dope dealer needs to transcribe the sales goals and interpret them in less precise terms. It may sound illogical to remove raw numbers from business, but you'll try anything once, right?

To do so, he has to use his boss-hood skillset. He has to think strategically, and convert his work into tactical actions that the employees can execute. To the dope dealer, he needs to find new turf and then hire more people he can trust. The dope dealer has to develop a system of vetting individuals to see if they're an undercover cop, and likewise the new hires have to follow tactical steps to make sure they don't get caught by the DEA. Do you see the workflow here?

If you ever watch AMC's *Breaking Bad*, you should be right on my level. The main character, Walter White, is a perfect example of a strategic thinker in the drug-ring who makes critical decisions for his tactical underlings to execute. He does a pretty good job of it, too, considering he has his own show.

Note

To reiterate, I'm 22 and I've worked for the best and worst bosses out there. Pending a varying degree, they tend to fall in these categories. If you don't recognize your boss in the above list that tells me one of two things: either you're really lucky, or you're working for a new breed that has yet to infiltrate the workplaces of modern America. Either way, send me all the gory details on LinkedIn---please!

Corporate Ransom Notes

As simple as the above tactic (interpreting strategy into execution) may be to implement, I witness a perplexing implosion of the principle during everyday work life. Instead of receiving interpretations from superiors, you get direct demands. I call them corporate ransom notes. Some companies even hire people for the sole purpose of reminding the middle managers that these ransom notes exist. They push and shove with phone calls and site visits, doing anything their inside-the-box brains can think of to apply pressure. The problem isn't in their communication, however, but their lack of realistic cogency.

Enter: Caribou Coffee

I used to visit a particular location in Atlanta because my girlfriend worked there and I really love their coffee. It was also a great place to hack away at this book and it just so happened to be nearby my house. Put those elements together and you have me, a raging fan. But given my inside connection, I learned about the not-so-pretty management tactics they implement.

Specifically, they call a district manager every few hours to report sales. Sometimes they fall short of a quota, such as selling three oatmeal snacks instead of five. Sound the alarm. And just as the district manager records the sub-par numbers, corporate's radar starts blinking. This is followed by a nasty message to the district manager. Call it the "bad egg" warning. Finally, the district manager contacts the franchise and demands to speak with none other than the store manager. After a minute of shuffling duties, the store manager is available to speak and her vernacular changes to "yes sir" as she's told the oatmeal is selling at less than stellar quantities. Corporate ransom note delivered.

Sidebar: the coffee shop recently went out of business. I'm now digging Octane Coffee (Grant Park) and Carroll Street Café (Cabbagetown).

So, we have a problem. Can't a business deliver sensible quotas without acting like a retard? Didn't the elementary tactics and snitching end in middle school? Allow me to introduce a theory. I call it The Jesus Method.

The Jesus Method

Consider this: Jesus was a real man. Scientists agree! He may not have been as perfect as the Bible claims, but he was certainly a philanthropist and has been made world-famous for over 2,000 years as a result.

So if you must, replace Jesus with Gandhi, Mother Teresa, Obama, or whomever you feel more comfortable.

First, an outline of Jesus Method characteristics...

1 | The manager practicing the Jesus Method ideology forgives mistakes

2 | He removes the idea that one person's mistakes are less critical than mistakes by another

3 | He consistently enforces personal values to the entire staff, even when there are no problems

4 | He is the most respectful person in the organization, and the fruits of his position are based on take-home pay, not a shinier nametag or a "Mr." name prefix

The Jesus Method ideology does not promote or require...

1 | Liberal rule enforcement

2 | Unmerited seniority (the old guy makes more / does less than the new guy)

I had such a manager in high school when I worked at Chick-Fil-A. As a Team Member, my responsibilities were to take and prepare orders. The owner/operator also preached a "time to lean is time to clean" mantra, so during downtime I swept the parking lot or made rounds in the dining room for exploded ketchup packets or crumpled napkins.

My manager was a recent college graduate who had worked various positions at Chick-Fil-A restaurants since high school. Everyone at our restaurant knew he was on some sort of management track towards ownership, so he was generally respected on that merit alone.

While we worked together I carefully observed his performance, figuring that was a good indicator of personal character. And while I wasn't being paid to judge, he passed my tests with flying colors. During large concerts at a nearby venue he was in the trenches with the rest of us, helping customers refill drinks and decide on dipping sauces. If the drive-thru turned nasty he provided extra support by going outside and taking pre-orders from vehicles past the loudspeaker. One time we had to stay late unexpectedly to clean the building for a health inspection. Without consulting us or waiting for complaints, he traded coupons with a local pizza chain for hand-delivered pizzas and breadsticks.

On the occasion business was sluggish, he would simply walk up to a random team member and volunteer them for a break with ice cream. It made us all work a little bit harder knowing there was someone with tangible rewards evaluating our behavior. But it also wasn't Big Brother. He didn't butt-in on conversations, sit in the back office on the surveillance cameras, or form private alliances with senior staff members. His comments were consistently candid, and he usually spoke to the entire group at once.

It's no surprise to me that this same manager recently achieved the coveted Owner-Operator agreement at a brand new Chick-Fil-A outside of Los Angeles, California. I'm sure he's doing well and will continue to grow both his management skills and his investment portfolio because he thinks strategically, translates expectations, and treats his teams with respect.

So get out there, start training your boss, and watch him begin to do the same.

Chapter 5 | Lessons in Naivety

The stupid neither forgive nor forget; the naïve forgive and forget; the wise forgive but do not forget.
—Thomas Szasz

The human spirit is a dynamic organism. By nature it is needy, whiny, lazy, and ignorant. It knows not when to stop asking, seeking, or becoming. It is the little engine that could. It is resilient.

Oddly enough, we seem to spend our entire lives taming the human spirit. It's as if we are inherently embarrassed by our natural tendencies. We go to college to become independent. We adapt quirky new lifestyles straight from self-help books to minimize expectations. We hang on to the words of motivational speakers, looking for new flavors of motivation to embrace and call our own. And daily, we devour information to shine light on the unknown.

If not practiced in moderation, it is through this truth-seeking process that some humans lose themselves. Think about the stories of celebrities and businessmen committing suicide. Or the religious extremists who murder innocent people.

Outside of death, how about writers, bloggers, app developers, and Internet marketers who would trade their souls for a good story or strategy? And finally, consider the familiar tune of a young girl rebelling against parents with premature pregnancy.

Suffice to say, the development of our human spirit is dangerous at best. To make matters worse, there is no timeless guide to achieving happiness or living life "to the fullest." With each new age comes a different set of struggles and societal trends. A teenager from the Roman Empire circa 1300 might have been consumed with the bubonic plague (which wiped out roughly half of the European population), while a teenager today might be more worried about popping facial zits the night before a school dance.

In recent centuries, the focus areas of human development have been less dramatic or, as we like to call, "primitive." Advancements in science, technology, and governmental infrastructure have not only ensured our basic survival needs such as food and water are met, but have also provided many luxuries and safeguards against huge disasters. But now that our bases are covered, we continue to pursue new development projects for the human spirit and beyond.

Instead of vying for shelter or companionship, we 21st century warriors wage battles against the voids of our human spirit by filling them with Botox, reality TV, and social media (to name a few). Because of this, it is imperative we maintain a healthy frame of reference for the human soul and what it ultimately struggles to become.

Among my observations of the obsessions of modern-day society, I've determined we are in love with children. We take more pictures of them than anything else in the world. We interview them in focus groups. We experiment with their minds through language programs, music lessons, and moral teachings. And most of all, we lecture them about how wonderful their lives are and how they shouldn't look forward to becoming one of us.

If nothing else, we obsess over children because they incite nostalgia and innocence. Many parents will say their children are their most prized possession, or go even further saying they are a driving motivation to live.

But to put it differently, I think we obsess over children because they symbolize the human spirit we've been taming our whole lives. Regardless of behavior, it is this element of humanity that makes children more pure than the rest of us. Their human spirit remains intact until we teach them to disregard it.

Best-selling author Robert Fulghum wrote the popular book *All I Need to Know I learned in Kindergarten* in 1988 in which he outlines basic life principles that serve as helpful guides for people of all ages. A few axioms include, "Play fair," "Clean up your own mess,"and "Don't take things that aren't yours." One critic from the San Francisco chronicle wrote, "Fulghum's stories about ordinary life remind us that simplicity lies in the sublime." This sentiment, simplicity in the sublime, is the very essence of a child's human spirit—*our* human spirit.

Therefore, throughout our lifelong quest for happiness, it's important we consider children-centric thoughts with the same vigor that we study advanced methodologies and philosophies. The following is a collection of child-like thoughts that can hopefully guide us back to our human spirit within.

Babies
A baby is born when two people love each other very much."
We adult folk know this just ain't so. Babies are born because people get drunk, make mistakes, or are trying to solve an argument. The few [and the proud]

pre-meditated parenthood experiences are far outnumbered by those who didn't take seriously the gift of life. So be different. Make choices that allow you to tell your kid they were created because you loved someone very much. I think their childhood will be a little bit brighter because of it.

Love

"Love is when a girl puts on perfume and a boy puts on shaving cologne and they go out and smell each other."

Love is arguably the least quantifiable and measurable phenomenon known to man. We don't know what to do with it, yet we cannot veer from it. We manifest within us the desire to love and be loved. It is simple, but not easy. It is also not convenient. Children are experts at interpreting circumstances by their face value—another tool of discernment unfortunately lost with age—and we should spend time trying to do the same. Why can't love just *be* a guy and a girl, smelling each other?

Life

"Listen to your brain; it has lots of information."

Modern-day culture stresses that we are victims of our own device. That some decisions we make are with our brains while others with our hearts, or things in our pants, or whatever. This self-victimization process leads to a lot of finger pointing and confusion. Most popularly I'm reminded of Christina Aguilera's hit song *Genie in a Bottle* when she remarks, "My body's saying 'let's go' but my heart is saying no."

All the talk about multiple personalities and ulterior motives clashing warfare within our hearts and minds and bodies is overly complicated, and we don't want that. So listen to your brain. It's not perfect, but it is analytical. It seeks a challenge. It begs for new content. If developed, it will keep you out of trouble and make your life easier. And the best way to develop your brain is to use it. Go figure.

Happiness
"Some people have a beautiful smile and when other people see it they feel happy."
We all know the phrase "happiness is contagious." The problem is we're all waiting to catch it from someone else, or some *thing* else (see: consumerism). Nobody wants to make an effort to manufacture happiness anymore since manufacturing gets a bad rap. We're told to share everything, including the guilt of others. But happiness is a pipe dream, and it won't present itself to us through others. Let's embrace the wisdom of grandparents everywhere and "pull ourselves up by our britches." If we start by smiling, the rest will follow. I read a wonderful eBook for 99 cents titled

Love Yourself Like Your Life Depends On It by Kamal Ravikant. Check it out at pinff.com/love.

Death

> The little boy seemed to accept Belker's transition without any difficulty or confusion. We sat together for a while after Belker's death, wondering aloud about the sad fact that animal lives are shorter than human lives.
>
> Shane, who had been listening quietly, piped up, "I know why."
>
> Startled, we all turned to him. What came out of his mouth next stunned me. I'd never heard a more comforting explanation. He said, "People are born so that they can learn how to live a good life, like loving everybody all the time and being nice, right?"
>
> The six-year-old continued, "Well, dogs already know how to do that, so they don't have to stay as long."

Chapter 6 | Magnifying Glass

"Excuses are the tools of the incompetent."
–Shanelle Gabriel

I'm rambunctious. A constant energy flows through my veins. When friends and colleagues take a lackluster approach to their latest projects, I try to get them excited. It's not my duty nor my business to tell anyone what to do with their life, but I feel a calling to encourage others to pursue with a vigor that which they're *already pursuing*.

Does this make sense? I'll elaborate.

I don't sleep during the day. Sunlight is limited, at least in respect to my lifetime. And I open all the blinds and shutters long before turning on a lamp. Piteous artificial light depresses me. We learn in Physics 101 that heat = energy. Thus, sun = energy. Use it.

I go to coffee shops for added focus even though my home Internet is stupendous. Like drinking, I don't listen to rap music until after lunch. Throughout the writing of this book I've spent $500+ on coffee and I didn't start brewing at home until the manuscript was in revision. Go figure.

Let's try again. I like to encourage people. Sort of like a motivational speaker, but on a smaller level. The level that's real, lacks Botox, and is totally *pro bono*. But being an avid likes-to-hear-himself-speak type, it's difficult for me to listen. I begin losing my mind when others speak if they aren't preaching relevance to my life or being controversially humorous. Some call it rudeness, a product of a bad upbringing.

A book I loved as a child, *The Toothpaste Millionaire* by Jean Merrill, provides an incredible burst of entrepreneurial inspiration. Although published in 1974, its basic principles of marketing and capital management are timeless—especially in today's trying global economic climate. The story describes a young kid turning rags-to-riches by developing a recipe for toothpaste. He starts selling in his neighborhood and ultimately goes on to build huge factories. After reading it a few times, I was convinced I would make its fiction a reality. I stole baking soda from my parents' pantry and from there it went downhill.

Quite frankly my product tasted like crap, and I couldn't buy supplies for a second concoction because I had spent my allowance on Pokémon cards. I pouted, telling myself "Failure isn't an option." But option or not made no speck of difference because failure was inevitable. I was without resources, experience and, most of all, common sense.

A few years later when I turned 13, my friends began skating. Not the 4-wheeled block joints at the local rink, but aggressive skating, with ramps and rails and punk-rock culture symbolized by t-shirt brands and crappy attitudes. Jumping on the bandwagon I begged my parents to invest in the hobby, insisting it would open doors to a new future for me, perhaps even a career. I watched similar aged skaters like Ryan Sheckler who were already pro and just a year older than me. My friends and I made a plan of action to get on his level. Our idea was to film "sponsor-me" tapes and send them everywhere our dial-up Internet would provide addresses to.

In a recent class I took on human development I learned that the primary difference between ability and aptitude is that abilities are achievements as a consequence of realizing an aptitude. How profound. But there's more to it than that. The most notable implication from this statement is that ability and aptitude have an interdependent relationship.

I once heard this concept described in reference to a kite and its string. The string allows the kite to soar and the kite glorifies the string. Without the string the kite would tumble, and without the kite the string would never take off the ground. There's a similar tension between our abilities and aptitudes. Think of the difference between kinetic and potential energy and how much you hated physics. Their sum is never greater than one. Regarding a piece of matter (or object), as one force (kinetic energy) increases, the other (potential energy) decreases proportionately. These relationships are intriguing because they demand rational over philosophical understanding.

When we ask ourselves to improve, and then wait for another inner voice to execute that request, aren't we really just forming relationships between our aptitudes and abilities? The aptitude is potential—otherwise wasted energy—like the string that holds the kite. And the ability? It needs aptitude to soar. Without aptitude it is stolen baking soda...a failed project. It is a useless resource, or one that never even existed.

Heuristics are quick rules of thumb. A few heuristics are much easier to remember [and embrace] than a hundred how-to guides or procedural steps. And when friends get down on life because they hate their jobs, hate waking up for it, or hate their paychecks, I ask them why they can't change. It's like asking a vendor at a flea market "What's the best you can do for me?" Force him to challenge and compete against himself. Likewise, when I ask a friend what he can do better, the worst answer he can provide is "nothing." That would be self-deprecating and only make the situation worse because humans need hope. If we haven't any hope left, what really is there?

Take a personal example from August 2009. I had been short-selling stock during my freshman year of college and was getting pretty good at it. After making a quick 500% return on Sirius Radio (they merged with XM), my friend James and I decided to visit Los Angeles together.

A week later we flew out west and had a great time, connecting with old friends and doing the typical touristy stuff. From beaches and famous restaurants to the Hollywood Walk of Fame and audience roles on reality TV, we did it all. And the whole time we captured memories on James' nice D-SLR camera. I wanted everyone back home to know where I went and what I experienced.

When we got back home, albeit out of San Diego because we missed our flight from LAX, the first thing I wanted to do in my exhausted state was check out our photos and upload them to Facebook. So my friend sent over the files and I started browsing. The quality was superb and I was missing

California already. I looked at the palm trees in the photos' backgrounds—just beautiful. I remembered the breeze and the beaches and the skyline. Beautiful. Mostly I enjoyed our smiling faces and recalling the memories we had formed just days prior.

Then I started looking at the focal point of the pictures: me. I was overweight and out of shape. Naturally I was in almost every picture, so I was ruining them. I was wearing clothes that no longer fit. I basically looked ridiculous.

Cue self-deprecation. There was nothing I could do. The trip was over, experiences made, and worst of all everything was captured on a high-quality camera. So I sat there on my computer. And I didn't tag a single photo. All my self-absorbed intentions of sharing a vacation to Los Angeles were ruined by the extra 25 pounds on my gut.

But soon I had a change of heart. I considered health. I thought about eating better. About exercising more. And I dreamed up a new, fantasy body for myself. It was lean. It could run 5 miles without sweating. It could lift a lot of weight at the gym, in front of everyone. And most of all, it looked great. Great at the pool. Great in a suit. Great in my thrift store Girl Scouts shirt.

I began running the same week. Every night, at midnight, I would push myself 2-3 miles around the Buckhead neighborhood of Atlanta. Summer was over, and with fall approaching the weather at night was perfect. Even the hobos under the bridge on Piedmont Road and I-85 had a swing to their step. The pounds began to fall off. Within a week I was down 5lbs and could already see my profile shrinking. I ate heavily after my workout, but treated the food as fuel instead of a reward.

Over the next 12 weeks I bought a supplemental drug called glucomannan from the Vitamin Shoppe, which is basically a dietary fiber that expands in your stomach. It helps digest food (keeps you regular) and also curbs your appetite. Combining the suggested 1-2 daily dosages with my midnight runs was magical: I lost 45lbs in 60 days. Find out more about glucomannan at pinff.com/gluco.

I won't preach on the health of my methods because doctors advise us not to lose more than 2 pounds per week. (I was losing almost a pound per day.) But I will say that the power of motivation is a force to be reckoned with. I have zero athletic ability. I hate running. I can't even *swallow* big pills. But I did it all anyway. Why? Because a fiery drive inside my heart said I could.

That same drive is inside all of us. We channel it the night before a final paper is due, or when we start a small business and pick up a second job to fund it. We draw mere ounces at a time to provide only the sufficient amount necessary to complete a task.

But what if we open the valves full-blast? What if we have the conviction to say to ourselves that "good enough" *isn't* good enough anymore? What if instead of 5lbs we lose 10, or shoot for an A+ instead of a B-, or go for a raise in June instead of waiting until December when "the time is right"?

I'll tell you what will happen. Like most life endeavors, we will either succeed or fail miserably. We will better play the hand we've got, or try [and fail] to be dealt a new one. And this is frightening, certainly. But we'll never know unless we try.

A motivational poster on the wall in one of my elementary school classes read "Shoot for the moon! Even if you miss, you'll land among the stars." And that's the point I'm trying to make.

Throughout my short life I've tried learning fluent Korean, becoming a sponsored skateboarder, directing a successful YouTube channel, and a few of those get-rich-quick schemes. And I failed at all of them without shame because at least I obsessed while trying. Much like this book. It would have never happened until I got a huge wave of inspiration in July of 2012 and rode it for the next 60 days. During that time I brought the book's word count up from 5,000 to the over 36,000 it now bears.

In April 2012 I had the opportunity to compete at the Global Student Entrepreneur Awards. A total of 42 countries participate annually, and I was one of 4 nominees from the USA. As luck would have it, the conference was held in my hometown (Atlanta). With just a few classes remaining until graduation, I used my senior skip days and had an amazing 3-day experience networking and listening to incredible speakers.

A comedian named Kenn Kington delivered the keynote address during the conference's opening ceremony. He combined humor with sincerity—my favorite speaking style. The essence of his speech was simple: we can't be whatever we *want* to be, but we can be what we were *meant* to be.

This sentiment, at its core, is exactly how I make waves with friends and strangers when I learn about their dreams and visions. Tim Ferriss calls them "dreamscapes," to suggest that we turn our unrealistic dreams into tangible and obtainable goals. Yet, we so often miss the mark.

As non-conformist as we think we are, we really do care what others think of us. We get excited about a business idea, and then reconsider after a friend tells us it won't work. We daydream about backpacking across Europe, only to be reminded by our rigid parents that it's way too expensive and we'll never be able to afford it. Haven't they heard of Maneesh Sethi and his brilliant travel-hacking tactics? Go to pinff.com/travel for his insights into the world of inexpensive travel.

The bottom line is that opportunities surround us constantly and they are rarely delivered in pretty boxes by FedEx. It takes a trained eye to label something a big break instead of a bump in the road. And that trained eye develops when we draw from our inner inspiration with excessive ambition and thereby convince our ultra-mom Volvo-picking-up self to do whatever it takes to be successful. Stop giving your mind free handouts and vacations! It's easy on Saturday afternoon but always comes back to haunt us Monday morning. The same adrenaline, dopamine, or whatever that we draw from to knock out a last-minute essay, can be harnessed without a burning need for survival. It can be accessed whenever you please, given a trained mind.

You see, opportunities are cold, heartless creatures with a lot of insecurity problems and daddy issues. If we don't take ownership when they expose themselves, they have no problem rebounding to someone else. But we were made for them, so take it. Please, just take it.

Recently I went out to dinner with my girlfriend. On the way out to my car in the apartment parking lot, we visited the dump and threw out a lot of my trash from the week. I was holding a lot of empty pizza boxes and couldn't help but smell residual fragrances of pepperoni and garlic.

When we got in the car, we began to deliberate which restaurant to patronize. I made a quick jab against Italian food by remarking, "I have too much pizza in my life and not enough steak." Needless to say we did not eat at a restaurant with a chef named Vinny. My point here is not to make you think of week-old pizza, but instead how a lot of us fill our lives with pizza when we could be filling it with steak. Note to vegans: this is simply a metaphor, not an op-ed piece on slaughtering animals (although they are super tasty).

Of course, sometimes it makes sense to eat pizza. After all, it's cheaper and it solves a lot of logistical problems when you're having a big party. But other times, it's nice to treat yourself to steak. Note to vegans: sub "steak" with "spinach salad" or "tofu."

You might be saying, "Well I can't afford steak." But that means you aren't thinking. You've just shut your mind off again. And we don't do that anymore, remember? We seize opportunities now. Those insecure creatures don't stand another chance.

Robert Kiyosaki is a best-selling author and moreover an incredible financial investor. In his ultra-famous book *Rich Dad Poor Dad*, he preaches on the subtle differences between a rich man's thinking and a poor man's thinking. While the poor man exclaims, "I can't afford it," the rich man asks "How can I afford it?" One man is making a statement and subsequently turning *off* his mind, whereas the other man is asking a question and turning *on* his mind. All of us need to do the same thing.

How can we afford steak? How can we afford a better group of friends, a better Saturday afternoon, or a better skill-set with which to pursue our passion? We do it by turning on our minds.

I'd like to hear about your dreams. I'd like to know if there's a difference in your heart between what you *want* to be and what you are *meant* to be. So please, reach out with your story.

Chapter 7 | Business 101

Cannibals prefer those who have no spines.
–Stanislaw Lem

Owning a business license does not make you a businessman.

At my alma mater there are a lot of *wantrepreneurs* running around (credit: Mark Cuban). They shoot business cards like Texas Hold 'Em dealers and think meeting new people is an art called networking. The management teams they operate are large, and anyone who plays a role in them is dubbed a "business partner."   With no initial investments other than data plans on their smart phones, these insults to entrepreneurship toss and hurl ideas around at countless theory meetings and rarely follow through with application. Nevertheless, those in between the hustle (such as myself) are forced to interact with said individuals, at least on occasion, because there is one valuable thing they do possess: big picture ideas.

I call these individuals "idea boxes." Have they plans? Maybe not. Ability? Definitely no. But their ideas alone can be extracted by people like you and I. We can turn them for a profit, use them to change the world, or sometimes both.

To foster this concept, I've started offering free advice for college students with startup business ideas. Over coffee, on a conference call, or in the bathroom during a special event, I absorb as much of their passion and instinctual business hunches as I can handle. Picasso (or is it Steve Jobs?) reminds us that while good artists copy, great artists steal. Everything we do to innovate is, at minimum, stepping on a stone of innovation from the past. Or so it seems that way.

After several months of pouring my heart out to local clothing lines, video production companies, and freelance marketers, I've realized how imperative it is for Idea Boxes to be paired with [actual] entrepreneurs. Without us, they've got destinations without directions. Visions without business plans. Bottom lines without P&L's (profit and losses).

Thus far my findings have been copious. Michael Gerber writes in *The E-Myth* that as business owners, we are playing three key roles: the entrepreneur, the manager, and the technician. We start businesses as a technician who's sick of working for "the man." Once involved, we have no idea how to manage our workflow and escape the long, tedious hours that only a bad technician's funnel would create. Then comes out our manager. They delegate work, train employees, build systems, and handle administration. But that's not enough for growth. Hence, the entrepreneur. This personality innovates and dreams, pushing the manager to better bottom lines and the technician to more efficient methods. According the Gerber, to be ultimately successful we must put equal emphasis on all roles.

In that respect, Idea Boxes are 100% entrepreneur, 0% manager, and 0% technician. This deadly combination earns their name, but you can see how they are useful to actual entrepreneurs like us. We are more dynamic—a better mix of the three imperative personalities. So we listen to their ideas over coffee, on conference calls, and in the bathroom during special events. Get it?

Next, I've concluded that getting any business off the ground requires an incredible salesman. Usually it's the sole proprietor of the venture, but in rare cases you'll find partners who aren't completely incompetent. I've worked with others in the past and always felt like I was babysitting them. As civilians we were friends and equals. In the business arena, however, the victor was clear. And that's why I don't do 50/50 partnerships anymore. There is just no such thing as a 50/50 relationship; either you do more of the work, or you do less. And that's OK. But you should each be compensated accordingly.

Anyway, to make any money and sustain your business, you have to "Sell, sell, sell!" Word of mouth is beautiful, but the pre-requisite is existing customers. In the beginning, then, you have to *become* your sales pitch. You have to be a relentless self-promoter because the product is *you*. And when you hear about entrepreneurs pouring themselves into startups, it's because they're pouring themselves into their startup's sales goals. Getting that first customer, then the next. And each step along the way, quantifying which methods of procurement work best, and documenting them for the future sales person who will [to some extent] replace you. Now, on to the nitty gritty.

How to sell the F*$% out of everything:
1 | Charm
2 | Know-how
3 | Reason

Charm
This does not mean being attractive. I have never achieved that status. It is simply a culmination of learned skills and attributes.

It takes confidence to walk up to a frat house and ask for a glass of water. Or pop the question for a girl's number at the bar. Even the ability to give a presentation in front of a class or board of directors takes confidence, a primary ingredient of charm. Scientists in Korea are doing numerous studies right now to discover a hypothetical "Charm DNA" combination which they hope will provide quantifiable insight to the phenomenon of charm.

While they keep searching, you should too. Think George Clooney (with a little less cologne).

Know-How

Don't go around selling stuff you aren't passionate about or can't offer more than a memorized sales pitch to explain. And by selling I mean a lot more than pushing a product and a price. I'm talking about selling yourself. Selling a vision. Then projecting that vision from your spreadsheet to the prospect's heart. Convincing them that they *need* something, not that they should *want* it. Because when you get in the business of cars, you aren't selling cars. You're selling a status symbol that the prospect can show off around town. You're selling sex, speed, and an adrenaline rush. You're in the business of happy and you always should be, whether it's cars, fast food, or Girl Scout cookies. Know it. Own it.

Reason

Aggression is one thing; it entices excitement and demands a response. But you can't demand a sale. That's holding someone hostage, taking all their money, and telling them it's all right because you're "letting them live." While one salesman persists to make a new friend, or client, or certain hair-do come to fruition, another man tries something new. It's about avoiding insanity by monitoring what works and what doesn't. Michael Gerber, founder of E-Myth Worldwide and small business consultant extraordinaire, insists that we quantify everything we do in the vacuum of business. Quantify the efficacy of one greeting, or tone, or color, or shape of a sales package: the first word, the spacing on the pages, the thickness of the page—everything. Quantify different test groups and analyze which combination of variables worked best. Quantification is reason. Quantification ignores hunches, instinctual feelings, and otherwise nonsensical rationales to marketing problems. Quantification is the cornerstone of reason.

It's a given, then, that behind every successful startup (fancy word for new business) there is a wonderful salesman. It could be a person, an inbound marketing algorithm, whatever. Bottom line is, a startup needs oxygen (revenue) to continue breathing (growth).

But when you become (or create) an incredible salesman, you need to apply your skills in a particular way that resonates with the startups of modern-day society. They aren't the same as startups from the past, and here's why:

Old Startups

Suits

Scary investors

Board of Directors with formal meetings

Close relationships with local government

Complex management hierarchies

False appearances (Think: looking bigger than you are)

New Startups

Shorts/t-shirts/whatever's comfortable

Scared co-founder/investor/maxed out credit card

Email threads looping in friends with good ideas

F*** the police attitude/philosophy

First name basis culture

Two degrees of separation between employee and founder

I love the trend in new business to look small. The word "corporate" has recently garnered such a nasty connotation that even the biggest businesses in the world are pouring millions of marketing dollars into programs that will make them appear, well, less corporate. A mere 10 years ago it was prestigious to note the ", Inc." after a business name. Not anymore. Tech conglomerates now send personalized newsletters, clothing brands procure regional fashion lines, and beverage companies activate more small-town marketing events than ever before. I would know, as lately I've made a living giving stuff away for free.

I've also experienced the antithesis of this trend, having had the pleasure of working with a certain superior (who shall remain unnamed) who was obviously from the "bigger is better" school of thought.

Let me explain...

I spent 8 months in 2011 launching a coworking space in downtown Atlanta. We started with a huge, unfinished room that lacked even bare necessities like plumbing, electrical wiring, and so forth. Not coming from a background of construction, I was pretty overwhelmed to say the least. As time passed and my project deadlines were met I got over my fears and was somehow chosen to draft plans for the millwork in our café. Next thing you know, I was hiring sub-contractors and meeting with the fire marshal to discuss occupancy permits.

Sounds good so far, right? Well, here's where that old-school startup mentality kicked in. Somewhere near the project's end, I pushed myself back into the type of work I do best: branding, tech, ad copy, and price modeling. So I built a basic website for our company and then started creating alias emails for everyone involved. Naturally, I used our first names followed by "@xxx.com." Within hours, however, a superior insisted I change our emails to first initial, last name, like rkulp@xxx.com. He said we needed to "appear bigger."

There's another dynamic shift in new business that plays along the "less is more" ideal. Our society is increasingly becoming more minimalist, which is yet another affect of the 2008 financial meltdown. Our wallets, common sense, and most of all modern day opinion leaders are screaming at us that we don't need more stuff. We should stop consuming. The mantra gets tied into environmental concerns, inflation, and even currency speculation, but the core essence of minimalism is freedom from distractions.

In December 2011 I got really sick. I drank an off-brand sports beverage that was 1+ years past expiration. It was a dumb idea but I figured the airtight seal would make null the estimate. I was wrong. Within hours of getting home, I started feeling nauseated and sick to my stomach. My appetite was gone and I had a high fever chills. Long story short, I spent 5 days moaning on the couch, going in and out of light sleep. My body had a strong compulsion to go to the bathroom every 20-30 minutes, and from my unofficial tally I probably sat on the toilet about 125 times that week. Needless to say it was a miserable experience. My problems finally subsided when I made an appointment with the doctor and was prescribed special pills and Ginger Ale.

When I arrived back home, I experienced a new feeling of disgust. But instead of manifesting in my stomach, it was all around me in my living room, bedroom, and bathroom: clutter. I had trash, trinkets, knick knacks, trinkets for the knick knacks, and so on. And by clutter I don't just mean "stuff." I love stuff: my phone, computer, TV, guitars, and some mementos. Clutter, rather, is stuff that has no place or purpose, like an unlit candle on the mantel. Some extra pens on my desk. Five appliances on a tiny kitchen counter-top. That's clutter.

So I allowed my addictive personality to take over and I frantically began to put old items, instruction manuals, worn clothing, and even trivial things like extra pencils or Scotch tape into large black trash bags. Within a week, I had disposed of 25 bags full of stuff. Some of it was donated to thrift stores, neighbors, and my roommates. Other things I managed to sell on Craigslist and Amazon, like guitar pedals, DVDs, and even a laminator.

To fuel my fire, I started reading up on minimalism. For a list of my favorite blogs and books on the subject along with a more detailed personal testimony visit pinff.com/minimalism. I found motivation to continue downsizing by observing the dramatic testimonials from ordinary people across the country who were doing the same thing. For a while, I even went psycho-nuts when I got on the ATAD (a thing a day) bandwagon which suggests we should rid ourselves of one belonging every day. This may seem difficult, but it's actually a soothing exercise. Without realizing it, we actually consume so much crap that we are constantly collecting more things, even without making purchases. It's in our nature.

My next step was to consolidate like-minded products. For example, I donated my toaster because I already have an awesome toaster oven. I went the all-inclusive route. I got rid of 20+ unsharpened pencils because I have a few nice mechanical ones and a butt-load of lead.

Regarding logistics, I totally bought into the tote thing. Call me mom, but I really like having color-coordinated containers holding categorized objects.

One red bucket has all my music gear (cables, pedals, straps), while another blue tub has all my elementary/middle/high school year books. Some stuff I could never get rid of, and that's perfectly OK.

Aesthetically, the minimalist design principles are simple: clean surfaces, nothing on the floor, natural colors, and basic shapes. My coffee table has just one stack of 4 drink coasters. Hate those circle stains. My desk has my MacBook Pro, a lamp, and usually a few business receipts that I need to process in QuickBooks. In my kitchen, I keep all appliances that aren't used daily hidden in the cabinets. Yes, this includes my Magic Bullet. Beautiful device.

These little changes ultimately made for a significantly easy lifestyle shift when I moved from a house to where I now live, a small studio apartment. I wasn't anticipating the move (long story involving a thief who invaded our house and stole my Xbox), but regardless of the catalyst it's been a great new setup for me as a post-grad twenty something.

My new perspective as a minimalist in the realm of consumerism has led me to observe similar changes in the business arena. For example, flyers used to be hyper-comprehensive. If promoting an event, they'd even include where to park, visual maps showing directions from each end of the highway, and bullet point lists explaining dozens of activities and features. But these days, event flyers have a catchy one-liner of copy, a date, and a website. Clean.

Do you remember signing up for a new website account circa late 90s/early millennium? Usually companies asked for everything, even social security numbers in some cases. I distinctly remember creating blogs (Xanga), video game forum accounts, and eBay usernames. I remember spending 20 minutes filling out a full profile that included not only my demographic information, but also stuff like my favorite food and 1-2 backup email addresses. Then came 3 different activation emails that had to be clicked in a particular order or my account wouldn't be created. Nowadays, however, most online services just require a first name and an email address. This is a living example of businesses getting smarter by lowering the barriers to entry. In doing so, I say they are embracing minimalism. I like it.

Now that I've got you all worked up about minimalism, you're ready for a supplementary lesson in simple living. Each of these lifestyle design principles shares an overlap, but they are not one in the same. You see, we already know our world is becoming overwhelmed with clutter, but clutter is not limited to physical objects. If you have a clean coffee table but a ton of mental clutter, your life will remain stressful. So, before you settle on throwing away old clothes, instruction manuals, and electronics, consider a few additional outlets for stress reduction:

Mental Clutter

As you can probably guess, it's not plausible to completely eliminate our mental clutter without living in a cave and calling our volleyball "Wilson." We can, however, minimize our mental clutter. (See the overlap between minimalism and simple living?) In business, it's important to eliminate mental clutter because it allows us greater capacity to focus on work intensely prior to relaxation.

Remember the magnifying glass metaphor from chapter 6? With proper focus, we can make ordinary things extraordinary, like sunlight into fire. Use these strategies below to eliminate over half of your mental clutter today. Tips are taken from personal experiences and from one of my time management heroes, Tim Ferriss.

Email

You get too many emails. Department store sales, the daily deal mob coupons, new comment notifications on Facebook, and account updates for important institutions (bank, school). But you don't read them! You usually delete them without reading first. It's just a part of your life, you say. Wake up, check email, delete 90% of email, and respond to the other 10%. And it's sucking the life out of you. Your favorite show already has commercials. But at least you can hit the bathroom or find a microwave. There is no sitting out or ignoring the advertisements in your inbox, however. You have to delete them.

Hence, two activities that will save you time and sanity: filters and unsubscribe.

I love Gmail. I think other email clients suck and anyone using them is responsible for Global Warming. So do us all a favor and switch to Gmail. If you think it's too much work to switch your 37 accounts, think again. Gmail lets you import an entire mailbox with a single sign-in. Gmail will even import all the folders and contacts from your current inbox. Incredible.

So now that you have a shiny Gmail inbox, you need to take advantage of its best feature: filters. Make a folder for all your coupons, store sales, daily deals, etc. Call it "discount" or "coupons" or "miserly me." Kidding. To make this folder, click "create new label" on the left margin underneath your inbox.

Next, resist the urge to mindlessly delete emails from your smartphone. Doing this just suppresses the pain; it doesn't cure it. I'm no smartphone expert, but I've never been able to set up filter rules from either my BlackBerry or iPhone.

Instead, spend several hours creating these filters on a per-message basis. To do so, check the box to the left of an incoming message (that needs filtering), and then click the "More" button above all the messages. Click "Filter messages like these" and set up your parameters. I usually go with "Skip inbox," "Mark as read," and "Apply the label." Then just click the label /folder/category you've created for that type of message. You're done! Do this diligently for about a week and you'll have a much cleaner inbox. You'll still get all the same information, so there's no need to fret if you're a pack rat. It just won't be right in your face.

Second, the coveted "Unsubscribe." I'd wager there's some information you never care to receive. But you feel too lazy to log into a website and change your contact preferences. Well, to that I first say "tough." But I'm also here to say it isn't as difficult as you might think.

Believe it or not, those email blasts you get on the daily from Macy's or Wells Fargo fall under a ton of regulation. There's a board of directors, a bunch of bureaucrats, and of course the good old US Government. Most of the time, you can unsubscribe from annoying email newsletters with 1-2 clicks, starting with the "unsubscribe" button at the bottom of the email. It's very rare (these days) for a login to be required to change email preferences if all you want is to remove yourself completely. So unsubscribe, unsubscribe, unsubscribe. Do this for about a week and you'll rid yourself of even more mental filth.

Junk Mail
Your home address, ever since your inception, has been whored out by the masses. The Internet especially has provided an outlet for information-scraping pimps and their software to easily track

you, no matter what precautions you take. There's really no reason to bother with PO boxes, de-listing services, contacting USPS, or removing your name from Sporkle.com. (Although if you haven't done so already, it's still good to go do that.)

You can, however, abide by one easy rule that will minimize the time you spend looking at, complaining about, or handling your junk mail: review mail once per week.

No more everyday routine of shuffling through mail after work as you walk inside your home. You're likely to separate a couple useful-looking coupons in one pile, a bill in another pile, and the eye-blistering colorful advertisements in a third pile. Stop doing that. Put all your mail in your kitchen's top-drawer—you know, the previously labeled "junk drawer" that you finished cleaning out during your minimalist sweep. And don't give your mail the time of day until you're bored out of your mind on Sunday night.

Schedules

This is a "do as I say, not as I do" section of the book. One of my biggest weaknesses is saying "yes" to all sorts of requests, ranging from tangible opportunities (i.e. camping trips) to obscure crap (i.e. sponsored networking events). I think I also spend a disproportionate amount of time helping people move into new apartments or houses. If you help people move a lot, you are probably a "yes" man, too.

If there is one thing you can do to zen-ify your life, it's to create a hassle-free schedule. This doesn't mean not making appointments, it means making them hassle-free.

Start by consolidating your to-do's. Allot 2-3 days maximum per week for grocery shopping, lunch appointments, checkbook balancing, and housekeeping. If you find yourself feeling empty during the off-days, fight the temptation to create busy-work. Any drug therapist will tell you that experiencing withdrawals is the first sign that your actions are working.

Regardless of how lazy you are, your brain isn't used to being completely relaxed. It seeks engagement during all waking hours and the best way to train it otherwise is to do absolutely nothing for short bursts of time. Some people call it meditation. I've always thought that word was a bit creepy and cultish myself.

Institutional Accounts
The double-edged sword to living in the Information Age is that everything of value is stored within an

institutional account. Our email addresses, bank reserves, and credit cards are all examples of necessary institutional accounts.

But what about unnecessary accounts, or accounts that can be consolidated? Here are a few ways I've cleaned up my accounts.

Opted out of loyalty programs (with exception of SkyMiles)
Consolidated bank accounts/credit cards (checking, savings, and credit accounts now with one bank)
Bought an HD antenna (no more cable bills)
Changed utilities like Internet, gas, and electric to month-by-month basis (no contracts)
Opted out of paid subscriptions for business (DropBox, QuickBooks, Fraud Protection, etc.)

When determining the best accounts to keep and which ones to dump, the proof is in the pudding. Do you swipe the same couple of cards for every transaction, or put the same magazines on the same stack in the same drawer? If so, start downsizing the others. The worst that could happen is you click "sign up" one more time in the future. Need motivation? Just think about all the money you'll start saving with fewer bills.

High-Information Diets

By nature, humans are curious. Children plague their parents with the "why?" game, seeking each additional piece of information available to make resolute the piece of information they were told before it. As grownups we still possess the insatiable yearning for knowledge, but instead of asking our parents we resort to Google, or celebrities, or religion.

Luckily, a child's quest for further information is often short-lived. This is thanks to the all-too-familiar phrase, "because I *said* so, *that's* why." When we become adults, however, there isn't an authority figure in our life who spends time shutting off information valves or telling us "because I *said* so." As a result, we are prone to filling our minds with lots of extra garbage.

"Where exactly does this irrelevant data originate?" you might wonder. We get it from articles on MSN's home page, IMDB, television, and even Wikipedia which adversely impact our judgment and ability to learn more important things. Not to mention that when we take in useless information, it becomes increasingly difficult to decipher the pieces that actually matter from the other tidbits that are conversation-starters at best. If you ever met a know-it-all, you met someone who reads up on lots of useless information.

A trained mind focuses on special areas of interest, both for work and leisure purposes. In doing so, the trained mind has more room for new interests and thoughts that will add value to the trained mind's life. Put simply, a trained mind enjoys clarity.

I once had a boss who literally began shaking his head and waving arms if I spoke to him in a conversational tone. He would insist over and again that I make my point clearly and quickly. If I didn't, his shaking would resume. The most accurate illustration of his behavior would be watching an epileptic have a seizure. Or better yet, watching Kramer on *Seinfeld*. While my boss' method may have been a bit extreme, I learned a lot about getting to the point. I also subsequently realized that most everything I know has absolutely no tangible value. Like pointing to a blank map of the USA and knowing where every state is located.

I wouldn't go so far as saying that we should *only* learn things that have clear monetary or relational benefits. After all, we're the same kids who once got slapped for asking "But why, mommy?" I will say, though, that we absorb far too much information for our own good. If you spend a week reading less, watching less, and generally consuming less information, I guarantee you will achieve a new level of clarity. Whatever that means to you is all right with me, but please try it soon. Nobody likes a know-it-all anyway.

What's the Point?

After all that talk of saving time, reducing stress, and learning less, you might be wondering why I think those ideals relate to business, much less Business 101.

My logic is simple: starting a business requires communication skills, focus, motivation, and a stress-free atmosphere. While I could give you all the business tips and tricks the universe, Internet, and my pint-sized career has taught me, it probably won't do you a bit of good without getting these fundamentals down pat. After all, do you really want to start building a house without a blueprint? So yes, there is a method to my madness. I *will* find that "on" switch in your mind, gentle reader. Just make sure that if you haven't yet picked up what I'm laying down, do re-read the first several pages of this chapter.

Feeling relaxed? You're now halfway through a spa day. Your worries washed away in the shower, your possessions (both mental and physical) have been exfoliated to reveal the real you, and you've sat on the yoga mat long enough to think with clarity and purpose.

For the next bit, I want to briefly discuss some of the foundational principles to starting and running a successful business. Most of these I've learned the hard way, although my teachers really did make a valiant effort.

To start, let's talk numbers. Yes, the dreaded field of accounting. As the idiom goes, "In accounting, there's no accounting for taste." And that means you've got to learn to like it.

Accounting 101
Besides my ranting opinions and biased observations, you also need to know the basic principles of business if you're going to score any money. This is a quick discussion about business principles in accounting, along with common mistakes usually associated with each term. They should help define/refine your business plan (if you've got one) and save some headaches during the startup phase. To the guru readers, consider this a relaxing mental intermission.

Profit vs. Contribution

We're lectured on this in Accounting 101 but I don't think professors do a good job explaining it. They're more concerned with Acme Co. selling widgets than a guy named Tom selling funny t-shirts. So scratch that horrible experience from your memory.

If you sell a funny t-shirt for $20, and the materials cost you $5, you're left with $15 *contribution*. You did NOT just achieve $15 profit. Rather, the contribution does just that—it *contributes* to your profit (aka bottom line). There are other costs to consider, such as the time it took to make the shirt or the shirt's wear and tear to your screen print machine. For example, you might need to pump $50 of oil and soap into your silk screens every month to keep them printing in top shape condition. You might also have to drive 50 miles to pick up a box of new shirts or vinyl. But you can't possibly split those costs into a per-unit amount. Instead, those costs become your overhead; they are a culmination of random expenses that you inevitably pay for every so often, and are most commonly aggregated to monthly amounts. They fall into categories like travel, office supplies, and miscellaneous expenses. They are incurred regularly, almost like a subscription service. Your $15 contribution helps pay for them. That's why if you sell a dozen shirts for $20, with a $5 cost of goods associated with each, your *contribution* margin (contribution / selling price) will remain static at 75%, but your *profit* margin will fluctuate. Cool?

Business Model
According to Michael Scott, "there are 3 types of business: manufacturing, textiles, paper..."

Don't be fooled by oversimplifications. Depending on your Miriam Webster preferences, you might classify businesses by industry, location, tangibility, or something else. Personally, I define business by their business model. Put simply, a business model is the method by which a business makes money.

In that regard, all businesses are defined as either service-driven or product-driven. For many small businesses, it can be difficult to determine what really drives your revenues. For example, are your customers paying for 4 hours of your time with a photo booth (service), or are they paying for 250 printed photos of their party (product)? To understand whether your business is product-or-service-driven, you have to first determine your *core competencies*. This term is often thrown around at corporate-level strategy meanings, but it does hold value for us mere mortals.

For something to be a core competency, it must pass two criteria:

1 | Superior (in some way) to the competition
2 | Not easily duplicable by the competition

If you sell t-shirts, you've got gobs of competition. Everybody sells t-shirts. So what do you do? Lower prices? That would give you an edge over the competition, but would be short-lived. Everybody can lower prices. But what if you find a silkscreen fabric from a boutique retailer in India that transfers images with higher clarity than an American wholesaler's products? Then you would have a core competency.

So you have a core competency (or two, or three) and need to further define whether you are product-or-service-driven. In the t-shirts selling what-if analysis, your competency (quality) can be applied to either model. For example, you might print other company's logos and sell them wholesale for corporate events. That's service-driven. Or you might hire a graphic designer, create original art, and retail the shirts to college kids. That's product-driven. A third direction might be a mixture of corporate work (big word for "paying customer") and indie retail (euphemism for "poor customer"). But you will still have a primary revenue source. You will not produce an equal 50% of profits from each selling strategy, or business model; either your product or your service will primarily drive you. Make sense?

Cost of Inventory

This is a more obscure accounting lesson, but I'm touching on it because I think it lacks understanding if not combined with other business principles, such as cash flows and return on investment (ROI). So here's a combination of the three.

1 | Cost of inventory – opportunity cost (what other things you'd otherwise have) of holding some items for anticipated sales

2 | Cash flows – logistics of money; strategies for actually having cash regardless of profits and revenues

3 | ROI – most important measurement for deciding whether your business is worth it (more later)

Imagine you have a brand new warehouse. I mean gobs of space. And it's in South Bend, Indiana, which has some of the cheapest warehouse property in America (60 cents/sq. foot). So you're pretty stoked, and ready to fill it up with stuff to sell. Now comes your budget. You've got $100k and you want to sell all sorts of things, from slap bracelets to unlocked iPhones (for T-Mobile customers). Naturally you make projections and decide to order different quantities of each item, in proportion to how many (and how quickly) you'll sell. A week goes by, and everything is now stored inside your warehouse. You've still got gobs of space, so what the heck. After selling your first iPhone, you replace the empty shelf with another iPhone. And because you're smart, you put the cost of goods into a separate account and then pocket the profit (remember, *contribution* is not *profit*). But now you're back where you started. You've got a shelf full of iPhones. So you sell another, buy another, and pocket the profit. It's like you can't make any money without spending money and it seems impossible to get that big break. That's because you're holding too much inventory.

Here's a better strategy. Take the amount of money it costs to order a new batch of iPhones, what their per unit cost is, and how many days they take to arrive. Then look at how many iPhones you sell (on average) per day. If you sell 5 iPhones per day, and it takes 5 days to deliver a new batch of iPhones, then you need about 25 iPhones in stock at all times to have uninterrupted service. That means if you have 25 iPhones on Monday morning, you should order more. Then, by Friday, you'll have 5 iPhones and a new delivery of iPhones. Calculated correctly, this is called the *economic order quantity*, or EOQ.

So if you started with 100 iPhones (because you didn't know what the hell you were doing), it's better to pocket the profits for the first 50 phones without putting anything back into reorders. Then, keep all the revenues (profits + cost of goods revenue) for the next 25 phones and use it to order 100 more. Or 50 more, or whatever. Just don't keep too many on the shelves, or you'll never cut yourself a decent paycheck. You'll just a million unlocked iPhones for T-Mobile customers.

Next, cash flows. When you sell the iPhones, you probably won't be lucky enough to get paid right away. You can always set up E-Commerce to funnel customers through a secure checkout, but that will have separate consequences like losing customers. Even if you use popular services like Paypal, money is often held for 3-5 business days before being transferred to your bank. And during those days, you're broke. You have no money for new orders, emergencies, or Indiana nightlife, because you've been pocketing all the profits. Thus, the need for a discretionary account, usually called *retained earnings*.

Retained earnings are a separate account with some amount of liquid (cash) that's used to 'buffer' the discrepancy between accounts payable and accounts receivable. Accounts payable are things you owe like rent, utilities, and other regular expenses. Accounts receivables are all the little outstanding invoices from every stupid customer who hasn't yet paid you. And you hate them for it, but that's business. Just know your accounts payable people hate you too.

Back to cash flows. This is really the art of having (ideally) a butt-load of cash at all times for irregular expenses and expansion opportunities. For instance, maybe you find a new iPhone supplier whose prices are 20% cheaper than what you're currently paying, but there's a 100-unit order minimum and the pipeline is only open for a week. If you don't have retained earnings, you won't be able to take advantage of the opportunity. So you've got to ask yourself: Is central-Indiana nightlife *really* worth it?"

The problem with most startups is that they don't aspire to practice good cash flow methodology. Any money left over is either scraped off the floor by the cofounders (and spent on frivolous celebratory crap) or dumped back into the business (printers you don't need, nice pens you don't need, another self-absorbed logo banner you don't need). If this money was put into a retained earnings account, however, the company would be much better prepared for benchmark growth. So suck it up on the front-end, and watch your business scale in the long run.

Lastly, return on investment. As I said, this simple measurement is really all you need to know in order to continue doing business or shut that crap down. For this bit I'll use a real-life example: Mylar Designs. I founded Mylar Designs in September 2010. We do pin-back buttons, magnets, key chains, and bottle openers. But our only focus is pin-back buttons. It's a muse business, and by muse I mean that it's low-maintenance, high return, and not at all definitive of who I am. And that's important.

Without any marketing efforts and very little admin (logging invoices, tracking inventory), I pocket ~$500-$1,000 monthly from 1-2 dozen active clients. The money is good, because 90% of it comes from re-orders. This means I don't spend time resizing art, developing new relationships, or performing customer service. I already have the customers, they already like the product, and my job is simply to deliver consistent results.

Given these parameters, all money generated by Mylar Designs (after paying cost of goods, $4 /month hosting, and $15 /month bank account) is profit. Specifically, it's spending money. Mylar Designs buys me groceries, fast food, Internet service, electricity in my apartment, and a few tanks of gas. And I get all of that in return for a few hours of work per week. And that's a good deal to me.

Down to nuts and bolts. I have a few button machines, each of which makes a different sized button. I can do pins with a 1", 1.25", or 2.25" diameter. That's it. And each machine cost me around $300, one-time. After buying other things like storage containers and supplementary equipment (die cuts), my total spending on permanent assets for Mylar Designs is around $1,200. And from that $1,200, I've generated over $18,000. About 60% of that is profit, meaning I've made $10,800 from an initial investment of $1,200. The return on investment is almost 10-fold. Do you see how that works? It's not about making $1,000 /monthly or $1mil /monthly, but about the return on investment. On the other hand, if my equipment had a heavier price tag (like $10k), I would have to note in my projections that it might take upwards of 12 months to break even. That's a high-risk situation that yields a tiny return on investment. Got it? Good.

Below a quick story of how I got Mylar Designs off the ground and in 70% automation mode. Feel free to skip ahead if you want to work really hard for your money.

In September 2011 I paid for all initial Mylar Designs button-making equipment with our first sale, from which I cashed the check before placing the order.

Not every business can be funded this way, but it worked for me.

After the first sale, which was secured through a former job connection, I needed ways to reach new customers. It wasn't enough to simply believe that buttons are the greatest, cheapest, trendiest, and most exciting way to raise awareness for a brand, band, or organization. I had to make other people believe the same things. And I noted that while the end result of all transactions would be a product (button), what we were really providing was a service (marketing). And what's a great way to win over a new customer on a service? Let them try it for free.

Thus, *Trojan Buttons*. I coined the strategy from the mythological Trojan Horse scheme wherein the Greeks used a huge wooden horse, disguised as art, to infiltrate the city of Troy. Once inside, they busted out of the structure and began slaying women and children. Score. Which brings a metaphor: business is war. But we'll get to that.

For Mylar Designs, the process is simple: identify a nearby business with a fun brand, find the logo online, and print several sample buttons. The last step is to drop them off at the business with a business card. The visit is always unannounced, and we don't stay long. I walk inside the restaurant/art gallery/clothing store, and greet the first sales person I see. I don't talk prices, I don't ask them to call me, and I definitely don't ask them what they think of the pins. I just tell them I live in the neighborhood and that I like to make pins for nearby businesses. Usually they ask immediately for my card, and that's when I present it. Never attach a card to your free sample—it's presumptuous. A moment later, I'm back on the streets with a smile. To date, this method converts about 1/3 of the samples to sales and costs only a couple bucks per business. Talk about a low customer acquisition expense.

That's enough about me. It's time to put key learnings into action. French author (forgive him) André Maurois famously said, "Business is a combination of war and sport." Besides the elements of winning and losing, I think this parallel holds true because war and sport both require strategy. And just like at your workplace, there are different people responsible for strategy procurement and strategic (tactical) execution. Let's go more in depth.

Business is War

I don't take credit for the correlations between business and war; after all, Sun Tzu wrote an entire book about it (which I haven't read). However, in my own experiences I've learned that there are 3 major similarities between winning a war and winning at business:

1 | Fight till the death

The fundamental problem of all businesses is finding new customers and retaining old ones. This is also known as "growth." To find new customers we already know it takes one thing: sales. It's simple, but not easy. I repeat, simple, but not easy.

In a traditional sales funnel, prospects are categorized as either "interested," "qualified," "in discovery," or "under contract." The age-old idea is that the more prospects you dump into the top of the proverbial funnel, the more converted customers will come out of the bottom. Put youthfully, if you ask a new girl out on a date every day, you'll get more dates.

Mathematically this makes sense, but it also ignores what marketing teaches us about target markets. Instead of pre-qualifying customers with demographics and sociographics, the sales funnel insists on weeding out bad eggs via self-elimination and burned bridges. A perfect example is receiving a telemarketer's phone call, during dinner, on a Friday evening, inquiring for the "man of the house" in order to sell a new sewing machine. Just wow.

Ever since the dawn of the Internet, we have become engrossed in what's known as the Information Age. We don't innovate manufacturing with new alloys but with Six Sigma data-processing software. We don't invent new forms of light with thousands of experimental trials but with computer-driven what-if analysis.

Therefore, it is our duty to embrace the tools available to us and pre-qualify customers with evidence already at our fingertips. For pointers, the telemarketer should have asked for the "woman of the house". Yes, gender roles still exist. Yes, that is part of the demo/sociographics marketing mix.

2 | Never Underestimate the Enemy
There's a reason POWs aren't automatically massacred by their captors. They have information, which as we already know is the most valuable tool in modern society.

And by enemy, I mean competition—the incompetent, overpriced, dishonorable contender in your industry. They take customers that should be yours, and then rape them with inferior services and bad experiences. If it doesn't piss you off, it should.

Ever hear someone say, "It's all relative?" That's how competition works with business. As much as you monitor the enemy's actions, they're likewise watching yours. Pricing models, branding techniques, sales pitches. Keep that crap on lockdown, or you're doomed. Your competition will whore out your website and free brochures like a freebie training manual. They don't care, because they have no souls. They're copycat, good for nothing, zero-innovation slackers whose end-goal is to piggyback your prospects and steal business when you look the other way. So stop underestimating them.

3 | Strategy of Attack (not of Defense)

Resources are limited. As you divide them, every decision will be a nuclear warhead vs. 100,000 ground troops. Quantity versus quality. I learned from my days with Red Bull that you can *make* impression or you can *own* impressions. A television commercial during the Super Bowl clocks 100+ million viewers, making a $3.5 million advertisement cost just 3.1 cents per impression. Optimal and efficient pricing, right?

But what about the 1 million drunk viewers who pass out during 4-minute commercial breaks? Or the 500,000 party hosts, who are busy reheating queso and checking on hot dogs? Fred likes them black but Sarah wants hers "just right." And worst of all, how about the 10 million children whose sole purpose in watching the Super Bowl is to stay up an hour later than their bedtime. You just never know how many of those impressions actually made an impact, much less converted to sales. Thus, the crucial distinction of impressions *made* vs. impressions *owned*.

Ammunition (A la Carte)

In business, like much of life, some people get a better head start than others. Like the cool high school kids we talked about earlier that have hot moms and fast metabolisms. Like the prodigy who competes in a spelling bee. Like the runners born in Kenya...

Some head starts are innate, others are just dumb luck. I've been a musician for almost 10 years, yet as a baby I had lots of ear infections and nobody in my family ever played an instrument. Who'd have thought I would be inclined to record and successfully sell a professional album? Much less when Sony Music heard one of my songs and flew me to NYC in 2010 for a private showcase with a talent scout? Oh well. My parents aborted that dream when they paid for my college education. In the meantime, you can hear the song that booked me the trip at pinff.com/song.

Anyway, I think usually we make our own luck. And as I've mentioned before, the most powerful modern day tool is information. Just add water.

Here are some tools I've found helpful in the business arena, no matter what industry/model/corporate-level strategy you choose to approach with your idea. They are a combination of learned, innate, and dumb luck. You know, something for everybody.

Personality
According to Myers Briggs, my personality type is ENTJ. As petty as it may seem, these 4 letters are indicative of a winner. Various household names with the same personality include Abraham Lincoln, Bill Gates, Julius Caesar, Aristotle, Sigmund Freud, Margaret Thatcher, and Peter Thiel. The most closely related (and popularized) personality type is called the "'Type A personality" which symbolizes someone who takes initiative, is competitive, and feels a strong sense of time urgency. While the term has been around for 50+ years, it does little for society. The reason being, there is only one major alternative: the Type B. And, as you can probably guess, a Type B personality indicates someone is not aggressive, feels no compulsion to meet deadlines, and is easy-going.

What a sham! Do you like being placed in 1 of 2 personalities? If not, take the Myers Briggs test at pinff.com/personality. I think you'll be shocked by the accuracy of the post-test analysis.

Looks

Hold up, this isn't an article in People Magazine about having a symmetrical face or a definitive jaw line. You don't need to be a model to score in business. But you do need to prioritize your looks. And no, I'm not even talking about body-mass index (BMI), upper/lower body proportions, or having ripped abs. When I say looks, I mean demeanor.

Successful business people sport a certain "look" that is sought after by those aspiring to be like them. This seemingly indefinable look exudes confidence, humbleness, and focus. When this leader walks into a room, everyone picks up that this person is probably "in charge". People assume this person gets paid more and that they have eyes on the back of their head, with which they are silently observing their subordinates' every move.

Maybe it's something about their stoic facial expression. Perhaps we subconsciously sense how much someone is turned "on" to their work duties, compared to the rest of us whose minds are wandering around after-work fantasyland. It's as if we can discern whether someone "means business" or is just there to pay the mortgage. But that's enough speculation.

As we've already learned, the old way of doing business is a dying breed. Our father's generation has a completely different understanding of what it means to be professional, innovative, compliant, practical, and so forth. There's nothing wrong with that, but until they all die or retire we're stuck in a type of limbo.

Here's another piece of advice to give you a head start in business. This is basically everything I've learned from 4 years of being in university marketing classes and working for global corporations. It's also an abridged version of the hundreds of articles I've read and digested from Twitter, the blogosphere, business case studies, and of course personal experience.

If you're only interested in having one takeaway from Business 101, let it be this next topic. You will either thank me later on your deathbed (and more importantly in your will) or I'll be anticipating a subpoena for destroying your dreams.

The Fourth Dimension of Business

Our world is composed in part by different dimensions. Practically speaking, every tangible object has 3 things in common—the dimensions of length, width, and height. But what holds them all together is the 4th dimension: time. For hours of entertainment on the dimension of time, I highly suggest the cult-classic *Cube* trilogy. It's a Canadian series (don't hate) of thriller films that started in the late 90s. Go to pinff.com/cube for more details. Anyway, back to our regularly scheduled programming.

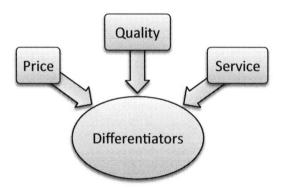

The first three dimensions of business are price, quality, and service. These are what your grandpa and his grandpa yapped about on front porches during heated discussions about Sears, Roebuck & Co. They are easily measured, much like length and width. Visit any retailer's website and you can compare every line item from features, pricing, and quality reviews with just the click of a mouse. But that just isn't enough anymore. Enter, the 4th dimension of business: Brand.

So what exactly is a brand? It's the personification of a company. If a company were a person, it's the personality and habits of that person. Neutron LLC defines a brand in their presentation *The Brand Gap* as "the gut feeling a person gets about a product, service or organization." For their entire [free] slideshow, visit pinff.com/brand. When I worked for Red Bull, our brand was defined by [human] character traits, such as "loves life," "anti-authoritarian," and "self-mocking." As is such, all Red Bull events and athletes are living, breathing representations of the brand they personify. And you know what isn't a brand? A logo. As they saying goes, "a logo isn't a brand unless it's stamped on a cow."

There are a number of reasons that the steadfast 3 dimensions of business aren't viable options anymore for differentiation. One being that in the 21st century there are fewer barriers to entry. More people can launch products and services (and with less capital) than ever before. Critics made similar claims about artists in the music industry after the rise of resources like Myspace, Purevolume, and most recently ReverbNation and Bandcamp. Everybody is a publisher. Everybody is a director. Anybody will sell you a car. Anyone can sub-contract jobs with an account on Freelancer.com. And the only way for a business to find salvation is, as always, differentiation. But it's not about pricing anymore. It's not about outspending your competition (see: viral marketing). Unfortunately for some, it's not even about having a better product. It's about branding.

It's been said that 2/3 of Apple's $600 billion net worth derives solely from brand equity. This means buildings, assets, patents, proprietary technology, sales, credit lines, human capital, cash, and projections combined are valued at half of the intangible—the brand. Let's take a moment to consider this so-called brand that makes Apple the most valuable company of all time.

We begin by examining the outlets most popularized by Corporate America into building brands and retaining companies. They are social media, blogs, sponsorships, marketing events, and advertising. Let's take a snapshot of these items.

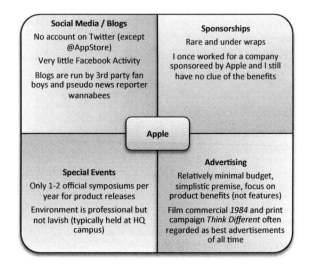

Social Media / Blogs

No account on Twitter (except @AppStore)

Very little Facebook Activity

Blogs are run by 3rd party fan boys and pseudo news reporter wannabees

Sponsorships

Rare and under wraps

I once worked for a company sponsoreed by Apple and I still have no clue of the benefits

Apple

Special Events

Only 1-2 official symposiums per year for product releases

Environment is professional but not lavish (typically held at HQ campus)

Advertising

Relatively minimal budget, simplistic premise, focus on product benefits (not features)

Film commercial *1984* and print campaign *Think Different* often regarded as best advertisements of all time

Brand Channels

If all this is true (and it is), how does Apple esteem such a valuable brand?

I think part of their brand is in *not* having a [by-the-book] brand. When I think of Apple and seek analogous historical examples, I'm reminded of the fictional Willy Wonka and his chocolate factory. Nothing goes in, nothing comes out. All information is need-to-know basis only. The effect is a quite literal microcosm of fiction: consumers recognize the logo, own the products, and yet know nothing about their production or procurement.

If you have a business, give it a brand today. If you haven't yet left the idea phase, add this element to your mix. I cannot stress enough the incalculable value that is derived solely from the fourth dimension of business: brand. Don't be like our fathers; don't be fooled into thinking that price, quality, and service will guarantee you a buck.

As Bob Dylan so famously sings, *the times, they are a-changin'*.

Chapter 8 | Visionary Loopholes

"Leaders are visionaries with a poorly developed sense of fear and no concept of the odds against them."
–Robert Jarvik

Technology changes our world at a break-neck speed. Within the past 100 years alone we stopped riding horses, lighting candles, and listening to real-life storytellers (except Dane Cook).

I'm just a 90s kid, but I still remember some of our world's most impactful pastimes, such as dial-up Internet and the brick phone. With each advance, consumers are left in wonderment while companies are already dedicating resources to the next best thing. What used to take a marketing research firm and dozens of intellectual consumers now requires only a single brilliant mind, like Jony Ive of Apple.

But what if it doesn't even take a brilliant mind? We all know the saying, "necessity is the mother of all invention." And we all need things. Or do we? Some economists don't even differentiate between wants and needs because most everything we have [and think we need] is unnecessary to sustain life. See: cell phones, email, GPS, Magic Bullet.

See, the way it works now is industry leaders imagine the next thing society "wants" and then hire Ivy Leaguers to develop and execute. We buy it all because it's shiny and then convince ourselves we need it after the fact. But you don't have to be an industry leader to imagine the "next big thing."

As an entrepreneur, one of my daily struggles is to ponder the next big societal waves and do my best to ride on top of them as they barrel down a pipeline of success and fortune. In other words, I try to capitalize on new and emerging opportunities. You know, *Carpe diem* and all that good stuff. While this picture I'm painting of the entrepreneurial quest is probably a familiar one to many—more like entrepreneurship 101—it's useful to recap the basics. This is one area (unlike 99% of college) where cramming everything you know onto a 3x5 inch flashcard won't be enough to "pass the test."

Do you ever have those ah-ha moments where a new product is advertised on television and you tell yourself "I totally should have thought of that?!" Simply put, that failure to act is what separates entrepreneurs from everyone else. It is the entrepreneurs who seize new ideas and turn vision into reality (excuse my romanticizing).

Some ideas, however, are perhaps too far reaching into the future. Everything is 20/20 hindsight, but people with good business sense are more apt to envision the future and prevent, if not avoid, many otherwise devastating mistakes.

One primary way to teach students in upper-level business classes (as I found out) is through case studies. A case study is simply documentation outlining a real-life business scenario which involves pivotal decision-making activity. General company information and market research that relates to the decision, such as competition and trends, is described in detail. A student's job is to analyze the data, formulate trend speculation, and report (concisely) all possible outcomes for every option including *status quo*. Don't you want to try one? Sure you do! Below is a quick sample.

Wait.

Don't like the terms "case study," "visionary," or "trend speculation"? No problem. I'll keep talking about them anyway and you can use my new phrase "societal loopholes" to sound "less corporate." And yes, I have a total love affair with quotations.

Here's our definition:

Societal loopholes (n) - phenomena we experience everyday—yet pay very little attention to—that aids rule breaking, practical inefficiencies, or unethical behavior

Case Analysis: WebVan

WebVan was founded in 1999 as a home delivery grocery service. On the backend it incorporated a .COM interface for placing orders and a complex warehouse and logistics network to execute the packaging and delivery of said groceries. Over $800 billion went down the tubes for the millennial service, and it's been dubbed by CNET the "biggest dot-com failure of all time."

Despite rave reviews from its limited customers, the service didn't appeal to a mass audience. It came out during a time when most people were just signing up for Internet service with AOL™, and the only affordable speed for middle class families was dial-up.

Enter: WebVan.

The website itself required a ton of data transfers in order to display product images and secure checkout procedures. With a myriad of results pages and bookmarking features, the site was a bit less-than-intuitive to new users, especially those who were using it from their first home computer. This inconvenient frustration played a particularly crucial role in the process of buying items like fruits and vegetables, since consumers like to a) feel for ripeness themselves and b) order in specific quantity arrangements.

Besides the website, WebVan also had to build out an entire network of robots and warehouses to store all of the food. In addition, WebVan hired thousands of employees to be "fetchers" of food from the shelves in these warehouses and prepare entire home orders for delivery. It was remarked by a company official early on that a 70 cent can of soup may have cost as much as $1.30 by the time it was taken from the shelf and packaged in a storage container for shipment.

A revolutionary website and array of food warehouses wasn't quite enough to secure WebVan's success, however. The final component to the WebVan system was an advanced distribution network consisting of many well-oiled, collaborative channels. Given the perishability of groceries, WebVan had to deliver products in refrigerated, insulated containers to the front doors of customers. They also had to do this within as little as a 30-minute window of time. The pressure on time was as much related to customer satisfaction as it was to the legality of delivering perishable food safely.

Quick recap of the actual businesses under the WebVan umbrella:

1 | Website
2 | Real estate development
3 | Distribution network

Findings

No need to go into too much detail or philosophy about the failure of our friends at WebVan, but to name a few...

1 | *Nobody* felt safe buying things online in 2001. (In case you're wondering, PayPal wasn't popularized until it was acquired by eBay in 2002. This ecommerce gap might have been a leading factor towards success.)

2 | Grocery giants Walmart, Aldi, and Kroger have an average profit margin of just 1-3%, according to Stacey Vanek-Smith of National Public Radio.

3 | Logistics efficiency is a never-ending project that takes years of trial and error. Perfect distribution is literally impossible. Consumer favorite FedEx Express could never afford to deliver all their packages

within a 30-minute window. Why did WebVan think *they* could?

Since I learned so much about this type of crap in my business classes, I'd rather spare you from any more of these types of samples. Instead, let's look at some fresh live bait. Let's get you on your way to becoming a visionary.

Here are some instances in our current day that I think could all become old news in a few years and have everyone saying, "I totally should have thought of that!"

Quick Sidebar

I promise to keep us on track, but did you know that Netflix started in 1997 with DVD mail subscription and had Instant Streaming available by 1999? I can't speak for everyone, but I had no idea what Netflix was until 2005 at the earliest. Wasn't that also ahead of its time?

The examples below aren't so much meant to be solved as they are a good start to get your mind a'churnin. Remember our ode to Bob Dylan in Chapter 7?

US Mail (security breach)

Never mind that it still takes a week to receive documents across country, a speed no faster than over 100 years ago, or that the entire system is going bankrupt. What I want you to consider is our emphasis on public mail boxes.

If you live in an urban area, you probably have a mailbox that locks. This might be right outside your front door or clustered with other boxes at an apartment complex. You feel safe about your mail because only you and the anointed courier have access to your space. But what about the suburbs where upwards of 50% of America's population lives? There are thousands of neighborhoods with millions of mailboxes left completely vulnerable to malicious activity.

We're actually guaranteed by the USPS that some mail gets lost. Some paychecks never make it to your door. But it gets worse. Some paychecks get delivered to the wrong address, perhaps your enemy's door. And we're supposed to just go with it. Oh well. Kids will be kids.

Unfortunately, these unintended beneficiaries can take our money, sentimental letters, expensive packages, unanticipated bill statements, and more, just by looking the other way and opening our mail.

It is truly a sore spot on the Fed's ability to protect private property.

My email provider makes me change my password every now and then. It also tells me where else my account has been logged into by IP address, data, and time. It's also free. Yet we keep sticking on stamps and crossing our fingers with the US Mail. What a shame.

Automobiles (practical inefficiency)

Have you seen the futuristic action movie *I, Robot* starring Will Smith? There's a chase scene where he enters a vehicle and forces it to abandon autopilot. As he begins driving the car, the computer warns him that he is being unsafe and will not have sufficient reaction time to respond. I think that's true right now.

Insurance is a mere deterrent to the real problem on our streets: *humans* drive the cars. We aren't allowed to have sharp pencils on school busses, but we can purchase 2-ton mobile missiles for transportation to work and leisure activities. This is strange, as 92 Americans die in car crashes every day. I don't hear numbers like that for school supplies.

I'm not saying we shouldn't be able to drive, or even that we should raise the age limit for a license or permit. I just think scientists could put more effort into transportation technologies aimed at having our cars to do more than just heat our seats and connect us to satellites.

Google has just created a prototype vehicle that drives itself, and they've demonstrated successful test runs around San Francisco, California. The car makes quick stops for unexpected traffic lights, brake-heavy drivers, and even jaywalking pedestrians. But alas, people are scared to death that a machine might someday make their high-speed decisions for them.

Pharmaceuticals (unethical behavior)
We feel sick, schedule a doctor's appointment, pay our crappy co-pay, reconsider our choice of benefits package, and after a 60-minute wait for a 15-minute visit we get a magic slip of paper. This is a prescription for drugs that with any luck will make our problems a lot more manageable. Moments later, we're on the way to the local drugstore and are freaking out about how much our next co-pay will be for the magic bottle of relief.

Think Jefferson Airplane's *White Rabbit* next time you're picking up drugs:

> *One pill makes you larger,*
> *And one pill makes you small,*
> *And the ones that mother gives you,*
> *Don't do anything at all*

Did you get all that? Let's recap: the technician takes our information and the script, and after 15 mysterious minutes of waiting we get our pills and another crappy bill. Do you see the loophole here?

Of all the legislation and restrictions in place in the pharm industry, the human element of delivery and pickup remains untouched. Even the final product (pills) are counted and put in containers by technicians, not pharmacists. It's sad to say, but Karl Marx might have had it right here when he criticized the Division of Labor ideal as worker "alienation," which leads to unsatisfactory work, lack of fulfillment, and ultimately depression. Quick question: do you want a depressed technician handling your pills?

Suffice it to say, opportunities abound. Some present themselves naturally, while others are simply marketing messages the world is telling us we need to know. So as we adapt to the lifestyles and technologies that feel right to us, let us always be on the lookout for the next big thing. Don't do it for you, don't do it for a paycheck, but do it for the world.

Hopefully these examples will get you started. There are dozens, if not hundreds more pressing case studies, ahem, "societal loopholes" to investigate. Pick one, destroy it with good analysis, and change the way we live.

Chapter 9 | 0210

*"It's like we weren't even working together, we
really became a family."*
–Every actor, on their latest production

We've all met celebrities.

We meet them at a high-profile party downtown, a
shopping center, a vacation spot, wherever. And we
wait for the perfect moment in conversations with
friends and family to mention our enlightening
rendezvous—which is really about *us*. We
exaggerate the encounter's worth and pass heavy
judgment on the celebrity's character, which we
base from 60 seconds of interaction.

One time I gave 2 hitchhiking strangers a ride to the
W Hotel in midtown Atlanta. They were on a
business trip from NYC, running late for their flight,
and the driver was [supposedly] waiting for them in
the hotel lobby. They asked me a million questions
along the ride to avoid awkwardness, which I
appreciated. When I dropped them off they gave me
a few bucks and a business card [to prove their
story], like I cared.

During our ride I got a 202 lesson; New Yorkers think
there is no other place like their city. That metro

transit authorities, ballistic hobos, expensive lifestyles, and late-night diners exist only on the island of Manhattan. If you ever find yourself in a conversation with a transplanted Yankee, be prepared for the disclaimer "back in New York" during 80% of the discourse. It makes me sick.

See what I did there?

So regardless of our presumptions about celebrities' lifestyles, looks, and most importantly beliefs and influence, it remains absolutely beneficial to still learn from them. After all, they have experienced things that we common folk may never even witness second-hand, such as exposure to prominent visionaries or brilliant artists. Most of all, they are a group of people in the public eye whose every behavior is analyzed and critiqued. So no matter their privileges and freedoms of stardom, they are walking on eggshells until death. And that's gotta count for something.

In my short time on Earth I've met several celebrities in all categories (A/B/C/porn) and while I won't say their names (I'll spare them the over-exposure) I will gladly deduce my key learnings.

First Documented Celebrity Findings (facetious)

1 | *Money Doesn't Buy Happiness*

We hear this pillar of so-called truth all the time, but I want to express my interpretation because it's different than the usual ones. First off, we usually hear this from poor people or those destined to be poor. They don't think money is important because they don't have it. What better way to avoid self-loathing than to perform what psychiatrists call "mental blocking"?

Secondly, we hear this from rich people who are already at a point of self-loathing. Either they feel guilty or are being arrogant and just don't know it. It's easy to say something isn't important when it's not a problem for you to have it. Do you see how we're stuck between a rock and a hard place?

Now for my take on the never-ending conversation. I think what people really seek (or should, anyway) is not a particular number on a paycheck but a particular lifestyle—one of choice, simplicity, and a few perks along the way. From Chapter 7 you may remember skimming over the benefits of simple living and a stress-free schedule, which in turn allows for all kinds of liberties. But do you also recall that there was no cost associated with those principles? And would you agree that on occasion, someone (perhaps even you) might already be enjoying a comfortable lifestyle given the chance to simply sit outside with a cool breeze, a drink, and a good book now and then?

So let's go back. The executive who makes a killing but hates their life and says money doesn't buy happiness is really saying they don't find fulfillment in spending their hard-earned money. And the reason they aren't fulfilled is because their lifestyle is at war with their paycheck. Familiar with the "work hard, play hard" chant? It is precisely the reason executives suck at life and hate everything.

By justifying poor recreational behavior with hard work, they also unknowingly justify hard work with the ability to play. The vicious cycle continues until they knock their bad habits or [more commonly] put a bullet in their head.

I've always hated the "work hard play hard" mentality and will continue to fight for my "barely work, relax a lot" mantra instead. Your money won't buy you happiness, but a lifestyle that fits your needs and aspirations certainly will. Some lifestyles require more money but others require almost nothing at all.

2 | *A person is a person is a person is a person…*

Stop idolizing your idols! Politicians, comedians, environmentalists, and authors all poop in toilets and have crappy best friend drama. You are doing a disservice to all celebrity-types when you place their average qualities on a pedestal. In doing so, you're suggesting they focus not on their talents but on Tweeting, directing, and becoming Scientologists. You are confusing them, and they aren't all that bright to begin with.

In fact, most celebrity-types are down-to-earth once you get them in a room without cameras or voice-recorders. (Keep in mind it's difficult making it to the top if you're arrogant.) And guess what? Eccentricity doesn't come with money or fame; it's a personal choice.

Applaud your heroes for a great performance of their skill, but not because they go to restaurants or fly Delta or have U2 on their iPod. What's on *your* iPod?

3 | *Cocaine is a Hell of a Drug*

In 2011 the world witnessed one of the longest celebrity train wrecks: Charlie Sheen. The car flew off the tracks long before the live media coverage, but we couldn't look away. The catalyst to it all was when Sheen got fired from his starring role on

CBS/Warner Bros comedy sitcom *Two and a Half Men*, but his episodes were far from over. Shortly thereafter he announced a comedy tour, and although it sold out in a record 18 minutes, it ultimately proved disappointing.

What's funny is that while our society holds celebrities in high esteem and goes to great lengths to protect them (lookup: "leave Britney alone"), we also show no discretion when using them as guinea pigs for social experimentation. Remember the bit about them not being super intelligent in the first place? By the way, go to pinff.com/britney for a good laugh and a feeling of concern.

Moral of this deduction: don't do drugs. Specifically, don't get high on false pretenses. You'll only set yourself up for disappointment. There are all sorts of people-pleasing activities on this planet and if you can't find them, you aren't being creative enough. The world is yours.

Chapter 10 | America

"I love America more than any other country in this world, and, exactly for this reason, I insist on the right to criticize her perpetually."
—James A. Baldwin

There's too much discussion about the whole world hating America. Personally I've settled the argument with a single metric:

Every day, more people attempt to enter America than leave it.

I refuse to become infatuated or defined by any single aspect of life, whether it's fashion, pop culture, my health, or where I live. I do, however, attribute much of my personality and human spirit to being American, which I think cannot be distinguished as a geographic trait. Rather, being American is a way of life. With it comes a unique set of philosophies and guiding principles that have consistently driven America's economy, military prowess, and technological innovations to new heights.

But it's not all Twinkies and *dum-dum* pops. I do also have a lot of beef with America. For starters, I hate everything about our federal government's irresponsible spending habits, and moreover I hate how this very spending empowers millions of citizens to be lazy. In essence, to be un-American.

As we all know in our hearts, change won't begin with a shouting match, holding up signs or sitting around hoping for the best. As Dalai Lama reminds us, "True change is within; leave the outside as it is."

The problem isn't the *government failing* to fix us. The problem lies in *our depending* on the government to fix us. In this sense, a government is merely a reflection of the values manifested within its people. After all, the government is just a bunch of people.

For me, this book is all about opening my *kimono*. I want to expose myself to others so they can pick and choose what ideals and opinions to subscribe to. Then, I want said people to reach out to me and collaborate on the project of life. And on a more basic level, I simply want to offer an entertaining set of anecdotes and key learnings. I have no intentions to profit, gain fame, or do anything otherwise labeled an ulterior motive, with this book.

That being said, I'm compelled to share a few of my more controversial convictions. (As if my belief in God wasn't enough, right?) Don't worry, I won't take you down a cerebral thinking path to explore the inner workings of brain (aka: what makes me "tick"). We're here to have fun and learn something about life, business, being a twenty something and all that good stuff, remember? Read on at your own risk. I'm a piranha. This chapter is independent from the rest of the book, as are freethinkers (you and me) from the rest of the world.

Red or Blue?

One thing a lot of people hate about me is where I fall on the political compass. I am a conservative. But I get called names like bigot, racist, and most often "ignorant." For the record, I have *never* called anyone these names.

I attribute my conservative values to the conscious effort to make decisions based on the principle in question. I learned at an early age that it didn't matter if misplacing my mom's tape was a $2 fix. What mattered was that losing someone else's property is shameful.

I have a set of moral convictions that claim there *is* a difference between right and wrong, and *50 Shades of Grey* is just a book, not a universal truth.

What I've learned about life, courtesy of conservatism:

1 | There is no substitute for hard work
2 | Live within your means, or increase them
3 | Love is composed by equal parts of justice and mercy

A common misconception among young American politicos is that Democrats are "for the working man" and Republicans are for the rich. But how did all the rich become that way? By working. Next, what follows is the all-too-familiar debate of "old money" vs. "new money." The idea is that old money is money left over from the era of slavery. As such, "old money" garners a lot of hatred by modern-day society and is usually regarded as a primary reason why it's so difficult to acquire wealth from nothing. Yet, as Thomas Stanley and William Danko point out in their bestselling book *The Millionaire Next Door*, over 80% of wealth today is first-generation.

Slow and Steady Wins the...Race.
Ahh, everyone's favorite dinner party discussion piece.

Americans can't seem to escape the idea of racism. It's fair to say we are completely mesmerized by racism, with our interest level being about as high as it is with children (see: Chapter 5). I say the "idea of" rather than the act of because I think a lot of racism hullabaloo is fabricated. I don't wake up, eat, travel, work, or sleep with racism in mind. But the mainstream media wants me to. It wants all of us to. The mainstream media (MSM) is the fuel to a never-ending fire of hatred and race baiting. And while racism is a human flaw (not a white flaw), America's MSM continues to dub white Republicans as universal haters of minorities.

What we don't hear about is how Republicans championed Civil Rights in the 1960s, or that Republicans founded all HBCU's, or that Republicans passed the 13th, 14th, *and* 19th amendments. Moreover, we certainly *don't* hear about how the Democrats formed the KKK. So please, do independent research. Your vote, and more importantly your moral compass, is much too important a force to be determined by CNN, Fox, MSNBC, or Obama's Twitter account.

Now let's get real. Our forefathers and their cronies did some detestable stuff. Their actions have forever tainted America's historical accounts. To some, America's history of slavery is completely unforgiveable. Cue: global and perpetual hatred. And I get that.

But how long are we to perpetuate the hatred and primitive ignorance of the last millennium, or the Aussies or the French? When will enough time have gone by that people in America can say, "Finally, we have a level playing field for success."

Some say "never!" They are the problem.
Others say "right now!" They have not identified a solution.

So I'll make this painless. If you feel the way I do and want to end the bickering and hatred about racial differences, begin today by accepting the facts and drawing sensible conclusions.

Embraceable Factoids
1 | Racism is a human flaw, not a white flaw.
2 | There is no such thing as "separate but equal" (see: HBCU's, special interest groups, NAACP)
3 | The faults of one's ancestors are not the convictions of one's character.
4 | The disparate lifestyle of another's ancestors are not the demise of that individual's future.
5 | Gandhi nailed it. "Be the change you want to see in the world."

Old America is Dead
No longer does a handshake seal a deal. Our litigious society certainly doesn't help, what with the

ambulance chasers and our growing welfare state. Beyond those reasons for blame, though, is the [collective and d]evolving mind state of modern day America.

The most accurate description of today's America is that we are living in the Age of Entitlement. We are born with outstanding invoices already addressed to us. The government owes us, our family owes us, and people we breathe on (or get breathed on by) all owe us something as we fight through life.

Naturally, then, we assume a protagonist stance on nearly everything. The world is conspiring against us. The traffic made us late to work. Our alarm clock failed to go off. The teacher didn't explain the assignment well enough. Boo hoo and poor me.

To pinpoint the origin of our entitlement age, we must examine the history of America's social programs. Verdict: social programs are government handouts/subsidies to less fortunate people (based on controversial measures) and funded by taxpayers. Sound harsh? I don't think so. But this is America, so feel free to disagree. Social programs have no intention of turning profits or even breaking even. Rather, they exist as a symbol and a privilege of living in a first-world society. It should be noted for the record, I'm proud that Americans have access to social programs, because their existence contributes to what makes us so (I think) great. But now for a bit of historical context.

Nationwide social programs began in the USA in the 1930s with the catalyst of the Great Depression. In 1932 the "Emergency Relief Act" was passed into law by President Franklin D. Roosevelt, which gave local governments $300 million to improve their infrastructure and provide for the needy. After several more provisions such as the Social Security Act (1935), Food Stamp Act (1965), and Medicaid (1965), our nation's people became fully marinated in a stew of government dependence. With the new bills came new angles of justification. The war made us do it. The baby boom made us do it. The farmers in other countries have better climates. Health care should be a "human right." Etcetera.

Fast forward.

Today, upward of 17% of America's GDP is spent on social programs. With the average household size being 2.59 people (2010 Census), this means roughly 1 out of 2 families are enrolled and withdrawing from some sort of social program. It's no wonder we grow up feeling entitled when we watch our parents demonstrate the same demeanor toward our federal government.

If you haven't noticed, I'm not preaching on the relevancy of any particular social programs. Obviously they exist for good reasons, or at least with mostly* good intentions (less those intended to garner votes). But Saint Bernard of Clairvaux makes it clear: "the road to hell is paved with good intentions." And so in my opinion, the difference between Old America and New America (current phase) is the distinction of entitlements.

Entitlement Age

Our country is losing its grip on the principles outlined in the *Constitution* and *Declaration of Independence*. The primary job of any acting president is to protect the Constitution, but today's leaders are more interested in writing a new one. They want to write a new constitution because voters are insisting that as our country evolves, so should our principles. So to win elections, politicians disregard their stated role of protecting the constitution and instead bow to the demands of mere folk. It's a vicious cycle, really, because to win an election (and affect *real* change) politicians have to raise money by promising small changes. Doesn't this sound like "buying" votes? Or bribery?

There's a real problem here, because if we want our politicians to be as squeaky-clean as we expect them to be, then we citizens have to practice the same integrity. Unfortunately, however, integrity is practiced only when it is convenient. You see, we expect our politicians to make promises. Big ones. And we should; I mean, that's their job, right? To affect positive governmental and societal change with taxpayer dollars and other resources made disposable only to an elected official. Go America.

But because of the tenets of our entitlement age, we hold proverbial knives to the necks of politicians and demand the world. Remember the "give an inch, take a mile" mantra from Chapter 4? They want to promise us better schools, and we demand teachers get tenure. They try to deliver cheaper health care, and we demand free contraceptives. It's kind of disgusting, really.

Let's not be mere folk. Let's not bother our politicians with petty programs and new social program iterations. There is a war going on out there, and quite frankly gay marriage is not part of it. We have China buying and selling our debts to rival nations for leverage. Soon they will own more than our debts—they will own us. One woman in China, Lou Xiaoying, found and rescued 30 babies in trashcans between 1974 and mid-2012. Ask yourself: do you want her country to own us?

War is Tricky Business

"Give a man a fish and you feed him for a day.
Teach a man to fish and you feed him for a lifetime."
—Chinese Proverb

This section gets its own quote. Yeah, it's that important.

"War" is such a buzzword. That's why in America we have a war on poverty, the unofficial name for legislation that racist former president Lyndon B. Johnson (D) passed in 1964 when the poverty level hit a record high of 22%. Looking back, he makes Obama's 15% poverty and 8%+ unemployment look like burned cupcakes.

In my opinion—and this is another strong one—if we didn't dub our socioeconomic problems a "war," nobody would even care. After all, it takes resources to "give a voice to the voiceless." But the only people fighting this war are poor people, and they're fighting for another welfare check. Also, they're winning. (Remember, we spend 17% of our GDP on social programs. And social programs don't produce wealth, they symbolize it.)

Let's not join in the games. Let's give needy people jobs, not welfare. Here's something my mom always told me:

Mom: "If you spent half the effort on _____ as you did on _____, you would be/have _____."

It's all about directed focus, which we covered briefly in Chapter 6's Magnifying Glass discussion. So fill in the blanks. If the poor/sympathetic/guilt-ridden people spent half of their efforts <u>fixing poverty</u> (jobs) as they do <u>suppressing poverty</u> (welfare), they would create <u>tons of jobs (prosperity)</u>.

It's not easy, but it is simple. And we all want a little more simplicity. So be American. Buy American. Or don't. That's what America is all about.

Chapter 11 | OCD

Compulsions are a lousy solution to the problem of having obsessions.
–Fred Penzel

We've all got a friend who's convinced they have OCD. The misunderstanding can strike at any moment, like after dinner as they scrub a dish clean beyond recognition. Or perhaps while at an antique store, where your friend shares their compulsion to straighten or reorganize trinkets. After their empty fit of psychosis, they slyly remark, "I have OCD; I can't help it."

What a load of crap.

Sudden urges to fix things, or change them, or simply the aspiration to be clean, are not indicators of OCD. They are indicators that we are humans, our minds are dynamic, and we appreciate ideal circumstances (whatever ideal means to you).

Quite frankly, I'm bothered when someone falsely claims they have a problem like OCD. I'm bothered because humans spend their whole lives trying to fit in, except of course when it's "cool" not to. It's like teens obsessing over an indie-rock band until one of their songs hits a billboard chart. What follows is a huge group of original fans retreating to the dive bars and starting a new addiction. The sucky thing is that the band now needs those die-hard fans more than ever! See: Fall Out Boy.

This bit is an attempt to speak for people with real problems who often get discounted by those who think it's cool to imitate. In doing so, the copycats cheapen the real problems of others and make it harder for real problems to get real help. See: insurance claims in the 21st century.

In this chapter I'm speaking specifically about OCD, but I hope you can apply my thoughts to other areas of life. The moral here, which I'll state long before the content, is that you should be true to yourself. Nobody else's lies will ever incur as much pain to you as your own.

Let me describe for you, the best way I know how, the essence of Obsessive-Compulsive Disorder. It is the conviction that the anxiety of not doing something [irrational] outweighs the embarrassment or inconvenience of doing it. The key word is "irrational," like avoiding cracks on sidewalks or stepping in the same patterns on stairs. There is no benefit to the behavior beckoned by OCD. And that is why it is a problem. That is why cleaning, straightening, and or articulating things are not pitiful side effects because they are not side effects at all. Rather, OCD is the little voice in our head that tells us if we fail to fix, clean, adjust, make symmetrical (relative), count, or contort our bodies, then we will die.

And we all know (even OCD'ers) that we won't die if we practice inaction against our inner demons of demand. But we indulge them anyways because the immeasurable, growing tension (anxiety) will otherwise overwhelm our thoughts and cloud our judgment if we fail to follow orders.

Next time your friends preach to you about OCD, ask if they can articulate the "why" behind it. Also, ask if they can elaborate on the cons of such a disorder. If they're only able to romanticize their "problem" with positive side effects, they're probably just another self-diagnosed phony. For if everyone had OCD, it wouldn't have a name.

Clinically speaking, I have 2 diagnosable mental plagues. One is Tourette's, and the other is a mild case of OCD. Tourette's is also a voice inside our head, and is often even more irrational than OCD. At its core, Tourette's is all about twitching. This could be a literal twitch like bending one's neck or a mental twitch like cursing 7 times consecutively. Fortunately my willpower to resist never deteriorated to such a level, but nonetheless having Tourette's earned me interesting nicknames while growing up.

My first nickname was Blinky. Remember when I skated with the older kids back in middle school (see: Chapter 2) and spent a lot of time discussing tricks, grinds, and new locations with my neighborhood punk crew? At the time, my twitch was a fast blink. I did a double-or triple-blink a few times per minute for about a year. Most close friends pretended to ignore it, while others who weren't raised as well made a constant spectacle of my ailment.

Soon, I trained my body out of the blinking twitch. But it came at a price—the opportunity cost of another twitch. So whenever I felt the urge to double-blink, I would instead tap my foot on the ground. Not long into this phase of habit killing, I had developed a new one. The blinking compulsion was gone, but now the voices inside my head were insisting I tap my foot (sometimes left, sometimes right) on the ground. While walking, while sitting, while lying in bed, whatever. Soon after I had to tap twice or thrice. Then I had to tap with more force. Finally, I was smashing my foot against the ground and making my knees sore.

If I were with company, I'd play it off by doing the same motion with the other foot. I figured symmetrical body motions were less suspicious, like I was working on a dance routine or sports play. I got so good at resisting my urges that I could make compromises with the voice inside of my head if the circumstances weren't ideal to let loose. If I couldn't stomp, I would put pressure on my foot inside my shoe, sometimes even curling my toes until they felt stuck. Mostly, though, I kept my habits symmetrical and continued to convince myself that doing things twice (on each side of my body) looked intentional and non-psychotic.

Ultimately, this led to my most recent stage of Tourette's — symmetrical twitching. Now, while I have an array of twitches (head nodding, clearing throat, squeaking particular pitches, etc.), the most important way to appease each of them is to do it symmetrically. If my nose itches, I scratch both nostrils with the same pressure. If I scuff my shoe on a protruding rock along a sidewalk, I scrape my other shoe with equal pressure at a similar angle. Do you ever pop your knuckles, back, or hips? I die a little inside as I change the position of each finger or side of my body. When I drive on major roads, I get into bad habits like centering my driver-side tires between the reflectors on the yellow lines. People honk at me a lot when I do that. If I hear a random high-pitched tone, like a beep on an elevator or from a backward-moving box truck, I have to match the pitch (via humming) and then run it through a couple arpeggios. When I get really into it I train myself to concentrate on a 3-5 octave series of pitch jumps, humming each in succession. If I miss a note by a half step or more, I restart the process. And yes, I do it around company, too.

Moving on, OCD. Speaking again about the little voice, it's pertinent to acknowledge that logic and reason do not relent against the inevitable anxieties of inaction. I'm a big fan of the idea that we believe things with different parts of our body, and that the whole gang does not share all our beliefs. For example, an amputee may understand the ramifications of his missing limb, the mind may have phantom-limb syndrome. Better yet, while an anorexic's body might be starving and begging for nourishment, the imaging department of the brain may see an overweight, unattractive person.

Similarly, while my college educated / resilient / optimistic / Type-A personality knows that I simply have bad habits and need to stop them, my selfish/childish/addicted personality knows to not be distracted by things that make good sense. And the little voices win again.

My point in writing this bit is to challenge you to be skeptical of those who cry the proverbial wolf. Our bodies, minds, and spirits are resolutely amazing and cannot be comprehensively quantified. While everything may happen for a reason, there is no solution to understanding reason itself.

For a closer look into the depths of OCD, read the essay below. I wrote it for English 101 during my freshman year of college, and it is a tell-all of the flavor of OCD that most severely affects my everyday life. Given the right blend of circumstances (the perfect storm), the events and mind-games described below take place in mere seconds.

Enjoy.

A Word is Worth 1,823 Words

So I'm sitting in a class. Any class, every class. The teacher says a quick line of instruction, or makes a note on the board. But this task is not one of the teacher's design; it is one of my brain's. The first thing I do is digest the meaning of the words: the *use* of them, so says my Critical Thinking textbook. Then, after I've done what is normally appropriate, and taken the necessary action of either copying down the note for myself, or placing it in a don't-forget-this part of my brain, I consider the word for its *mentioning*, so says my Critical Thinking textbook. In other words, I pick apart the word for the letters it's composed of, and discard any meaning that the word represents.

There are 26 letters in the alphabet, and if they were to be numbered, there are 26 numbers to the alphabet. A is equivalent to 1, B with 2, and so on and so forth. In my mind, every number and letter has its own place. Patterns emerge when the letters combine, but each letter has an independent task, and similar rules follow. Every odd letter (A, C, E, etc.) has a louder sound when pronounced in my head. To simplify this action, I call those the "hard" letters. As for the even letters, they have an opposite interpretation, which is to be quiet, or "soft." Why I use "hard" and "soft" as opposed to "loud" and "quiet" is beyond me, but these are necessary terms that cannot and will not be changed. In my mind, following the rules is much easier than trying to resist them.

Nevertheless, the teacher keeps on…teaching. I'm missing important details, and only half-consciously jotting down things to remember. With the processing sector of my brain at full capacity, all overflow goes straight to hold. As he continues to make points about supply and demand, he enunciates random words, like *"just,"* which can be used to take my mental progression to its next standardization.

I recite each letter individually, in the order given by the word's composition, and apply the suitable sound or pronunciation that goes with. For example, *"just"* is said j-u-s-t, but with accents given only to the two middle letters. This forms an interesting pattern, which in its style is known as inverse (soft, hard, hard, soft). There are other patterns, too, like soft, hard, soft, hard, or the reverse, hard, soft, hard, soft. To further show the possibilities, each response can be multiplied, as long as the word or phrase in its whole follows some sort of pattern. Meaning, there can be three soft letters, followed by three hard letters, as long as there are an even amount of both in the end. This, to simplify things, is the main key to it all: *evening out the word or phrase so that there are an equal number of both soft and hard letters.*

By now I've now missed approximately seven minutes of college—seven precious minutes of higher learning that I will never get back. I may never know the independent relationships that supply and demand share, or how demand differs from consumption, or even how my professor's doctoral degree shows no reflection in his English-speaking capabilities. It stinks not being able to have it both ways; it stinks that I can't appease my mind games while at the same time getting a good education. It stinks that the world isn't perfect.

When a word is imperfect, as words usually are, I have to use neutral characters to fill in the blanks, and to even out the soft and hard letters. Suppose my professor (in his broken English) says to me "I see your hand jumping, do you have a question?" My first rational, American loving response may be to correct his misuse of the infinitive, for my hand has "jumped" once, and is no longer "jumping." But that's too easy a task for my mind...instead, I embrace the word. I blind myself to see only the word *"jumping."* If I were to recite and make count of the soft/hard letters, I notice that there are three soft letters, and four hard letters. My mind, however, cannot accept this imbalance. It must have some sort of symmetry. So, to neutralize the word, I merely add a period. Yes, the punctuation mark. Because a period can be soft or hard, the distinction is up to me. Better yet, it's up to the word or phrase that it follows, because that's what dictates what it *needs* to be, to create symmetry.

The more obvious points of need are of course ignored, such as the *need* for my classmates to take showers, or that the police sirens heard through the windows *need* to stop blaring. These are petty problems not to be given the time of day, when taken into consideration by my mind's priorities. Rather, I observe my teacher's excitement as he draws perpendicular demand curves on a set of axis. He's engaging himself in what he's doing, so why can't I? Here's how.

To add to my own fun, I remind myself that letters said twice in a row lose their unique and permanent sound when said for the second time. Or the fourth. And so on and so on. Of course, with only twenty-six letters in the alphabet, the previously stated rule is important, because this situation presents itself quite regularly. To clarify, take the word that a classmate just yelled out: *"tall."* This was his answer to how the increasing demand curve can be measured. Clearly, this student is extremely bright. Anyway, after reciting the letters, one at a time, there is at first unease to its symmetry, or lack thereof. The pattern is soft, hard, soft, soft. But this is not so. Instead, the letter "l" actually loses its "soft" characteristic, and turns to the opposite, "hard," since it has already been said in the sentence or phrase. Therefore, the word *"tall"* is already perfect, in the form of soft, hard, soft, hard. No work is needed to complete the pattern, and periods or other punctuations are not considered. As said before, when this pattern is satisfied, my brain can resume its standard functioning. I can actually begin to process the thoughts, or mentions, of the words said or written by the teacher, and not just the use, or composition. Too bad class is over, though, and all I have written down is "Agenda." Whatever, at least the letters are perfectly balanced.

Now on to my next class, I see on the chalkboard the words *"speech test,"* which is wonderful, because now I can practice the system of steps in their entirety. The pattern found in the letters is (now using "s" for soft and "h" for hard) h, s, h, s, h, s, space, s, h, s, h. (Remember, the second "e" is soft, because it has already played its role of the "hard" letter the first time it was mentioned.) Also, when the letter "e" is used for a third time in the word *"test,"* it returns to its natural, or "hard", interpretation, because the cycle (soft to hard) has just been satisfied. Now, moving to the letter "t," the same rules apply. The first time that "t" is said, it stays true to the natural "soft" interpretation, for "t" is an even letter of the alphabet. When used a second time, however, it must be changed over to the hard version or interpretation. Next, after analyzing each letter, and taking note of the rules of double usage, we have one character left to decide upon. This character is the "space." After a quick review of our number tallies, one can remark that the pattern is comprised of 5 hard letters, and 5 soft letters. But this isn't good enough, because the words are separated by a space, and always will be. Combining the tail of one word to the beginning of another is plainly illegal, so one must make a further determination for the trait of the neutral character, the space. To do this, every letter can be read in order, and the gap will be filled with natural symmetry. In other words, s-p-e-e-c-h space t-e-s-t is read (again, with notation used above) h, s, h, s, h, s, space, s, h, s, h.

After looking over the pattern, it makes complete sense to declare the space to be a 'hard' character. But now one is again left with an uneven pattern of six hard characters and five soft characters. So, to provide final satisfaction for the meeting of the necessary symmetry, one must reach for another possible neutral character. This character, as first mentioned, is the period. By assigning the period after *"test"* to be "soft," one has entirely met the approval of the necessary pattern of letter equivocation, given the two interpretations used, and the rules that apply to their re-use.

All in all, it's been a great day of classes, with just a few notes, and a lot of things to think about when I get home. I'm thankful for what I got done today, and look forward to what I will inevitably encounter tomorrow. Perfection takes time, but achieving it is always worth the pat on the back my mind gives me after a good day's work.

Of course, the duty of equivocating letters with their numbered correlation is much more difficult and takes painstakingly longer amounts of time when a whole sentence is to be analyzed, but to go into that would require a book of which I have not yet been entitled the publishing rights nor the compensation needed to write. I guess that the motivation to persist in my thirst for flawlessness is more driven by the agony of not following the rules, rather than the pride felt when adhering to them. In other words, when unbearable can't be avoided, the best thing to do is make the unbearable of which you speak, more bearable. Or something like that.

Lastly, I often find myself re-arranging the words in a sentence, or more frequently, a paragraph, to the correct alphabetical order of the words. This can include the two sentence synopsis I record onto notebook paper, containing instructions on writing a personal narrative. Given the sentence "Use MLA format, keep the margins at one inch, and don't go over five pages," I follow all of the steps and rules mentioned above, and then turn the words into "and at don't five format go inch keep margins MLA one over pages the use," which places them in alphabetical order, and barely, *barely*, allows this narrative to follow both the underlying (and overlying) suggested rules.

This, I suppose, can be considered the last and final step of the mumbo-jumbo required to construct a perfect pattern out of words. Words that are worth 1,823 words.

Chapter 12 | The Executive Facade

The contest for ages has been to rescue liberty
from the grasp of executive power.
–Daniel Webster

Ahem.

We're all familiar with who makes up the cool crowd at any high school. Typically, it's composed of athletes, cheerleaders, and the fortunate sons and daughters of ex-athletes and ex-cheerleaders. But not just any sore loser is inducted into this hall of nonsense. See, the sport a cool kid plays must also have an intrinsic appeal. At my high school this meant football or cheerleading, and one of those isn't even a sport.

So you've got these kids, often times lacking in personality, and their opinions set the standard for what's "in" and what's not. I never was an official member of the crowd, what with my screamo band and bookworm lady friend, but I did have a close confidant who sat on the fence. And no doubt, it was interesting to hear his stories of what the cool kids were doing at post-game parties on Friday nights or during weekday "study sessions."

I've never been a gossip-seeker, but I kept an open ear to everything he shared because I found the leakage entertaining. The simple fact that he knew things I didn't gave him a sense of power over me. It was gratuitous at best, if not callous and petty, that he taunted me with images of what went on between kids who were "cool." My friend and I, let's call him Adam, shared this relationship throughout high school. In later years when college struck midnight he got extremely *fratastic*. I then informed him we were breaking up, cutting all our platonic ties. Kind of weird but it had to be done.

Consequently the stories stopped leaking, but by that time the cool kids were enrolled in community college and living at home with mom. Needless to say, their basement "get-togethers" were pale in comparison to even my geeky friends' dorm room parties at engineering schools. Ah, how the tables had turned.

What particularly bothered me about cool kids, though, wasn't their sports or privileges or Friday night activities. Rather, it was how materialistic and shallow they were. To them, personal rating was everything: the price of clothing a measure of their esteem, and the number of people who conjured images of intercourse with them a measure of their sex appeal. Somehow, possessing intelligence, a sense of humor, or any other agreeably admirable trait is merely a plus to the cool kid mentality.

Maybe you were like me, right in the middle of high school drama and barely hanging on to a few good friends. Or perhaps you *were* a cool kid, and now you're searching for the meaning of life. Whatever the case, acknowledging your place is important because it leads us to our first executive facade observation: there is a parallel trend between cool kids in high school and executives at a corporation.

Corporate Jocks

One of my favorite thrillers is *American Psycho* starring Christian Bale. In the movie he plays Patrick Bateman, a sociopathic investment banker.

As I recall, the audience never sees the Bateman character doing his job. Instead, we see an array of short clips at his office portraying Patrick Bateman and his colleagues comparing petty status symbols such as embossed business cards, new cars, and dress suits.

The same obsession with materialism (mentioned above), along with a primal, competitive nature is in the DNA of the modern-day executive. Italian suits, expense accounts, and BMW coupes are the new equivalent to Abercrombie & Fitch, parents' gas cards, and borrowing mom's car on Friday night.

Don't get me wrong – I'm not claiming that cool kids in high school become the Patrick Batemans of the world. Remember, they go to community college and live with mom. What I am saying, however, is that a parallel can be drawn between the mentality of cool kids and today's corporate executives. Perhaps this is how all the nerds who were once picked on by high school jocks return the favor. So if you ever think high school is over, think again. It's on loop.

Power and Distance

It takes a bag full of dirty tricks for modern-day executives (Corporate Jocks) to perpetuate their sense of "cool," or less euphemistically described: superiority.

As we already know when dealing with bosses, over time you will inevitably get closer to your superior and they will in turn grant you certain privileges, either in kindness or more likely through their subconscious. After all, they are human and so are you. That's how we are wired.

But corporate jocks don't want to form connections, they want distance. Why? Because the distance between themselves and everyone else is the primary measure of their power. If they get too close to a subordinate, they lose. Remember high school kids sitting at their own private lunch table?

I recently worked a weeklong gig with Samsung. I won't say what I did exactly but essentially I helped train wireless provider employees on new products and services.

There were a ton of executives at the event because naturally this was a very big deal to Samsung and their partners. Because of the high-profile nature of our work, I was under a lot of pressure to perform exceptionally well. Lucky for me, I enjoy pushing myself and I never let down my clients. (By the way, have you connected with me yet on LinkedIn? If not, go to pinff.com/linkedin to resolve that issue now.)

Anyway, during the event I worked with a lot of people. Most of them were responsible for giving me direction and assigning new tasks to keep me busy and productive. Again, no sweat, since I love being productive.

The problem is that while I *worked* with a ton of people of people, I never actually *met* them. Meaning, we didn't have a proper introduction. If you've ever been in this situation, you can probably imagine how awkward this made things when someone was screaming at me to do something and I didn't even know their name.

Here's how Samsung's executives skipped the introduction game (thus creating distance):

1 | I showed up at the event
2 | Some time later, corporate jocks showed up at the event
3 | Given my presence, I was mid-task when they began delegating tasks
4 | Within minutes, I'm following the demands of someone I don't know

Introduction Skip Game: accomplished.

This happens in all sorts of workplace environments. Sometimes it can even go on for months if an office is getting overhauled by a district manager or better yet, merged with another branch.

It wasn't that I didn't have time to shake a couple hands and say "Hi, I'm Ryan." It was that they didn't want anything to do with my identity. To them, I was a pair of hands and half a brain. My thoughts, opinions, experiences, and much less name didn't matter whatsoever. Their association with me, or lack thereof, was something carefully calculated...a game that must be played to win.

Too often, most of us fall victim to this type of treatment. When it happens, it isn't your fault; it's the corporate jocks'. Remember, they were once picked on in high school. This is the revenge of the nerds.

So how do we remedy this awkward situation? Well, we prevent it with another [more awkward] situation. Let's call it the Brute-Force Introduction Game.

1 | Show up to work
2 | Observe corporate jocks showing up to work
3 | Walk up to them and properly introduce yourself
4 | State your position and let them know you're more than happy to assist them (optional)
5 | Distance reduced. You win.

By simply taking the initiative to introduce yourself to those who don't want anything to do with you (just your product), the corporate jocks will enter a state of confusion. They will try to beef up the distance between you and them by drawing upon other tried and tested methods such as lowering their voice when you walk by or eating at a separate table in the break area. And that's OK.

After all, it's not like you want to *be* them. You just want to know the name of the guy who's bossing you around. Trust me, it makes work just a little less hostile.

Power Plays
I won't speak much to the why and how, but for your reference here are three power play moves that go down in every typical American workplace, regardless of the color on your collar.

1 | Emailing a boss' boss
DON'T do this. It shouldn't matter, but you might get fired. Happened to me before. Not a fun chain reaction to witness. It all comes down to "who's in charge" and whether or not someone can be responsible enough to manage their herd (you). Even if you have good reasons, go another route. Even an in-person quick talk might do more justice since there won't be a paper trail. Nothing sucks more than having your emails forwarded around, only to arrive back at your inbox directly from the person it was about.

2 | Delegating work to an equal colleague
DON'T do this. An old coworker of mine used to assign me tasks all the time. We both had the same title, privileges, pay rate, trust level with management, and so on. But for whatever reason he

thought he was my manager. On the flip side, if this happens to you, don't accomplish the tasks. The other person will learn very quickly that they can't depend on you to do their work. And that's exactly what you want them to think.

3 | [Consistently] taking long lunches

I won't comment on whether this is good or bad. Maybe you're the recent college grad who just doesn't know any better. Meanwhile all the middle-aged office drones are scoffing at you. Or perhaps you're the CEO and everyone has mixed emotions of "wish that could be me" or "he doesn't deserve to be CEO." Either way I suppose you could still be a recent college grad, but I digress.

Regardless of your reasons, the implications associated with taking long lunches are powerful. The message sent to coworkers is loud and clear: a) you value lunch more than the rules and b) you see your time as more productive than everyone else's, and c) you don't think long lunches are a big deal.

No matter the case or circumstance, being "that guy" who takes long lunches means you're contributing to the highly probable outcome of lowering office morale. Remember, a lot of office mayhem revolves around the "monkey see, monkey do" mentality. As others see you do it, they will want to rebel themselves. Or worse, they'll try to bust you for it. And since you don't want to work with a bunch of sore losers—much less get fired altogether—just be careful. Maybe sneak in a Fruit Roll-Up between conference calls instead.

Old and New

In Chapter 7 (Business 101) we did a quick recap of the differences between old startups and new startups. As you might recall, the discussion had nothing to do with types of businesses, price modeling, or where these startups find capital. Rather, we talked about the core mentality and principles embraced by the people *behind* old startups and new startups. We'll do the same thing here, but from the perspective of executives.

Head to toe, an executive is the powerhouse of business; the ace in the deck of cards. For aspiring business students, "executive" is the superhero fantasy answer to "What do you want to be when you grow up?" As such, it's important to understand everything an executive is, and likewise everything an executive isn't. Because like most dream careers and superhero fantasies, the truth is often exaggerated and half-told.

Old Executive

Anglo male, over 6 feet tall
Never a stray hair or an unpolished shoe
Three-piece suit and tie, always
Fearful subordinates, hot secretary
Type-A personality
Works 60 hours per week, takes long vacations
Strategically philanthropic (Corporate Social Responsibility)
Has a knack for public speaking
Travels heavily, misses family functions
Ignores distinction between "work" and "life"
Always climbing the proverbial corporate ladder
Steadfast work strategy and traditional, stubborn methods
Thinks "work hard play hard" is license to kill
Empty, stoic, unhappy

This character is a dying breed. He's a catalyst to expedient deterioration culminating in the economic crash of 2008, a time in which the classic American Executive became a demonized, cruel villain of nature: "Look at all these executives getting huge bonus checks while the rest of us can barely put gas in our cars..."

And their lack of diversity didn't help, hence the "male, pale, and Yale" intonation of the underground media. Thing is, while undoubtedly these individuals contributed much to growth and prosperity, and their departure from modern day business is acknowledged and appreciated, the time's come to make room for a new kind of business gladiator: a leader. You see, the old executive is a personality and a job title. But a leader is a philosopher.

New Executive
All shapes and sizes (including race, gender, religion, culture, etc.)
Comfortable
Resilient personality, nuances aside
Works whenever necessary, but not to a quota
Philanthropic by nature (enjoys helping people)
Misunderstood by many
Mentality of lifelong learner
Works remotely, telecommutes whenever possible
Puts more emphasis on "life" than "work"
Finds passionate fulfillment in work
Always tries new things
Works smarter, not harder

As you can see, the new executive has a completely different grasp on business, characterized by a holistic and philosophic approach. Yet, he still embraces hard work and persistence--values that remain consistent/constant with each generation of entrepreneurs.. The other flab falls by the wayside because the new executive knows that being clean cut and wearing Italian suits doesn't make someone professional.

New executives are emerging from dorm rooms, factory floors, and a lot of "oops" moments. By "oops," I mean that moment when an entrepreneur (you) is stricken with such an awe-inspiring idea that they can't help but develop it and see it to market. Not all "oops" ideas are successful, however. It's only the ones that are developed and brought to market that even have a chance.

The 21st Century Leader
Back in the day, "entrepreneurship" didn't exist.

You see, before all the corporate tax structures and globalization (specifically major transportation systems), just about everybody was a "sole proprietor" of some sort of business. Farmers are the staple case in point, as there were providing for communities across the country with little ripple effect on the rest of society. One guy raised livestock, another harvested grains. They traded and everyone was happy. Even the bartering system is parallel, because now we still barter but with dollars and coins. Running a farm took a lot of hard work, dedication, specialized labor, wisdom, and a bit of luck. Just like today's businesses.

Each proprietor from the past had one thing in common: specialization. For example, it made sense for one guy to only raise the livestock without having to manage the grain, too. Instead of seeking *independence* from other groups, farmers sought an efficient, steadfast *interdependence*. Simply knowing they had something the other people needed was security enough to continue focusing on one skill, product, or service.

Today's leaders are also specialized, and much like farmers from the past their skills are learned, not innately bestowed. Their natural personality type doesn't matter, nor does the projection of their voice or the look of their $5 haircut. Today's leaders are chameleons, adapting to others' personalities and mirroring the traits of those whom offer the possibility of an interdependent relationship that is mutually beneficial. And by relationships, I mean business deals.

In addition, a leader today celebrates family and has an excellent work-life balance. There's no need to go in to the office when today's leader has a VPN connection, a webcam, and cloud-based subscriptions for remote file and application access. For today's leader, altruism comes naturally and each paycheck is viewed merely as a means to sustain life and help others. After all, today's leader is a product of the help of others' before them.

There's a pay-it-forward mentality to first generation leaders, which bears a correlation to *The Millionaire Next Door's* observation first-generation wealth. The Gates Foundation has distributed over $25 billion in wealth to charities and causes, all because of the kindness of Bill Gates' heart. No corporation will ever understand that. Finally, modern-day entrepreneurial leaders are serial in nature because they continually dump extra income into new projects. And guess what "new projects" means? New jobs. And that's helping people.

In summary, today's leaders still share many traits of our so-called Old Executives. They are bread, not born. They are hardworking, self-made, and best developed by an environment which promotes equal chances to succeed. The family business (see: Government) is no longer a crutch to success, since success today means innovation and new ideas. Today's leader loves new ideas. Today's leader is simple. Today's leader is modest. Today's leader is you.

Chapter 13 | On Marketing

Business has only two functions—marketing and
innovation.
—Milan Kundera

Regardless of your political stance, I think marketing can only exist in a capitalist environment. By this I mean an environment where consumers have a fair amount of choice with respects to how they invest their hard earned cash. An environment where one can patronize a dollar theater instead of a Regal Cinemas, or shop at Salvation Army instead of Macy's.

Popular definitions of marketing are broad and dull, leading some to believe that those who engage in the practice have a low-skill, hippie nonsense profession. Steve Wozniak, co-founder of Apple, said in an interview with biographer Walter Isaacson that his father insisted he become an engineer because marketers (Steve Jobs) were a "bunch of phonies."

To understand marketing better than Steve Wozniak's father, the first step is not to define marketing as a whole but to look under the proverbial hood at all the moving parts. How are they interconnected? How are they in sync to create a streamlined powerful mechanism? A mechanism is a type of system, and companies with their crap together will call their marketing department a marketing system, or marketing "machine" (in the circumstance of automation). In simplified form, the primary components of a marketing system are sales, advertising, branding, marketing research, and campaign development.

Let's take a quick look at each and then bring it full-circle.

Sales

Here's where egomaniacs thrive. Prerequisites include a personality of 11 on the 10-point scale. It's kind of like a frat house. There's unnecessary aggression, obnoxious vocal tones, and a carefully formulated psychology embedded to meet goals and standards. Entry-level jobs in marketing are often sales-related, ranging from insurance to lead generation (sugar-coated in job descriptions as "client development").

Sales, unfortunately, is perhaps the necessary evil under the umbrella of marketing because it is the most quantifiable aspect of a marketer's efficacy. To make matters worse, corporate America provides only half-assed lessons. They teach us to *build* relationships, yet sales is actually the capitalization of relationships we *already have*. Roman philosopher Seneca defines luck as what happens when preparation meets opportunity. And that's sales. Can you tell I'm not a fan?

Advertising

Another dirty word on the marketing checklist. Dubbed "spam" years ago, advertising continues to struggle for a foothold on Respect Mountain. Evening telemarketers are an easy blame, since nobody really wants to buy an easy-to-clean rotisserie chicken spit after taking their first bite of mom's famous meatloaf. Advertising is like religion. There are countless tribes who will argue every aspect of advertising's purpose. There are gobs of research studies performed annually to measure whether advertising actually makes a difference. Even Sergio Zyman, former VP of Coca-Cola, once said that, "advertising, as we know it, is dead."

The guys in *Mad Men* might romanticize the industry a bit beyond its actual status, but there is a hint of truth to the breakthroughs and glorifications of brands that Don Draper presents:

Good ads are awe-inspiring, bad ads suck.

The essence of all advertising is communication. Advertisements communicate a message about a product, service, or cause through a variety of mediums, each with its own best practices.

Some ads are obnoxious, and others are iconic. Think about the 1990s "meow meow meow meow" cat food jingle. Now think Coca-Cola.

New media is emerging daily, thanks to the Internet and a bunch of fed-up college students. I wrote a paper in school about how the Y Generation rejects traditional advertising. We reject it because we see through a traditional ad's intentions: buy buy buy. Our generation is adopting a much different mentality towards consumerism. We are being taught (and rightfully so) that more possessions do not equal more happiness. Because of this, traditional ad tactics only reinforce our tuning out from typical marketing messages. But with smarter consumers comes smarter ads. Example: Have you seen OK GO's music videos that sponsor State Farm and Chevrolet, all under the guise of a cool Rube Goldberg experiment and a music video? If not, check them out at pinff.com/okgo.

If you must, accept advertisements as another necessary evil. They are the fuel to the rest of the marketing fire (if they work) because advertisements drive sales which ultimately pays for engineers (who scoff at marketing budgets).

Branding
We talked about this in Chapter 7, Business 101. Bottom line, brands are the newest dimension to

success in business. Nobody wants to talk about branding (except the people who "get it") because everyone thinks a brand is just a logo, or an abstract social media campaign, or a color scheme on a website. But we know better than that.

Brand building is a slew of activities executed both internally at a company's HQ and on the streets through customer reception and word of mouth. As a company, it is nearly impossible to build your brand. Rather, it takes the efforts of everyday consumers (your target market) to make a brand come to life. Advertisements don't build brands; they are just a form of communication. Doing builds brands.

Marketing Research

The only class I dropped and took twice in college was MK4200, Marketing Research. From day one I couldn't stand the quantification of every variable affecting a consumer's purchase decisions. Just because people say they'll buy something doesn't mean they will. Throughout my semester exploring this topic, I struggled a lot with the idea that psychology can be quantified. After all, that's what consumer behavior really is.

I do, however, believe in giving credit where credit is due.

Marketing Research is the activity of gathering and (more importantly) analyzing data about market place trends. Potential analysis goals from a marketing research perspective might be determining target markets, suggesting pricing models, or evaluating competition.

A lot of marketing research is theoretical, meaning it is done with the potential for a product or service to come to fruition. Essentially, it is a form of insurance for investors who are scared out of their minds at the prospect of liquidating assets for the sake of a startup. Marketing Research is like a pill prescribed to convicted visionaries that helps them sleep a little better at night. It is not, however, a sure-fire predictor of the future. All the marketing research in the world cannot unravel the mystery of human motivation. Just when you think you've figured out what buyers want, they pull the rug. Consumers are a fickle bunch, and marketing researchers need to stop ignoring that.

Campaign Development
This is the fun part. This is where all the activities and departments (remember Acme Co?) come together and create an ultimate mission for any given product, service, or cause.

A marketing campaign is an outline of the strategic and tactical approach that an entity intends to follow in order to achieve specific results. Those intended results could be $100 million sales, 10 million impressions, or perhaps just 1 new hire. It all depends.

To craft a well-balanced campaign, marketers get together and focus on each aforementioned channel of marketing. Some channels may be ignored (not funded) altogether or they might all be harnessed for a comprehensive and multi-faceted approach. But no matter what, social media guru Erik Qualman reminds us in *Social Media Revolution* that "Good companies listen first, [and] sell second." (For his videos in full context, check out pinff.com/revolution.)

Remember the strategic work we talked about in Chapter 4 (Terrible Bosses)? This is where your boss comes into play. He might be a jerk to your brand team, but he may also be a stellar organizer of marketing armies and top-down strategies. Think about it.

Some of the most innovative products in the world wouldn't have made their debut if it weren't for a killer marketing strategy. Take Netflix with their free 1-month trial. How about Facebook with the invite-only referral system (early 2000s)? And most recently The Snuggie, with its simple "buy-one-get-one" approach? The common thread here is that simplicity promotes effectiveness; truly, this is marketing at its finest.

Why Products Don't Sell Themselves

A lot of young entrepreneurs are prone to thinking that if they build a product or service that has unparalleled features then the word will spread like wildfire and business will be booming. "Build it, and they will come." But this just isn't the case.

Unfortunately, there is a gap among consumers' perception of a product's *features* and a product's *benefits*. This is why some people need Facebook but don't need a great vacuum.

To effectively market a good product, there must be a strong marketing message that does justice to both the benefits and also the features. I separate the terms benefits and features because while features are product- or service-specific, the benefits are consumer-specific. For example, one feature of the iPad is the touch screen. To a 2-year-old, the benefit is the intuitive nature; to me, the benefit is not having to clean earwax out of a tiny keyboard. Make sense?

Next, products must have a transformative power: they must turn their users into ambassadors for word to be spread. To sharpen this point's edge, replace "ambassadors" with "evangelicals." For example, let's say a really great lottery game comes to your town. They don't do any mainstream advertising, but you find out about it while walking by their big office building. You buy a ticket, and you win. You buy another ticket, and you win again. You're starting to watch your back, paranoid. You're concerned that others might catch on to your favorite new gambling habit. You're never going to tell a soul, because then you would decrease your chances of winning. So while this new lottery is your absolute favorite service in the whole wide world, you'll never tell anyone about it. Hence, the need for consumer incentives.

The lotto paradox doesn't belong only to probability for monetary gain, however. For *every* product (or service), there must be a positive incentive for a user to endorse and refer the product to someone they influence. But the benefit doesn't have to be as blunt or costly as a cash payout or a thank you letter from the CEO. It just has to give the user a warm fuzzy feeling inside. (Did you ever refer a friend to Facebook in 2005/2006 and feel like a social champion?)

Viral Marketing
This form of marketing has essentially been manufactured by the Internet. Until the day we all

die, the Internet will likely remain the fastest medium of communication by which information can be spread.

For this reason, the Internet is quite possibly the most valuable resource a marketer can harness.

It doesn't take a multi-million dollar budget and a Super Bowl placement to tell the whole world about your product. It just takes something extraordinary and novel, like a skinny attractive white chick rapping to a hip-hop artist's hit song. (See: Karmin, courtesy of pinff.com/karmin)

It goes without saying that I can't write a guide to viral marketing—nobody can. And that's the point. However, regardless of the medium (video, written, verbal, imagery), there are common trends across all content that makes it go "viral."

5 Trends of Viral Marketing
1 | Viral content is value-adding (meaning humorous, entertaining, informational, strange)
2 | Viral content sparks discussion (in the form of comments, social networking, imitation parody, etc.)
3 | Viral content is accessible (usually free, search engine optimized, keyword friendly, easily shareable)

4 | Viral content is time-sensitive (often based on a current event or at the brink of a social trend)
5 | Viral content has no clear agenda (important to note when attempting viral content creation)

When content goes viral, it can be the best or the worst day ever for the content's creator. While PSY may love the recent acclaim of his sensational hit *Gangnam Style*, other people (i.e. Rebecca Black) might not be so peachy about their overnight celebrity.

The truth: humans love a train wreck-particularly one in slow motion. We'll watch/read/do something over and over again just for the guilty, sick pleasure it brings us (if not for anything else). After all, who doesn't love being spoon-fed a feeling of superiority? If you can create viral content that a) provides consumers this feeling, while also b) protecting the content's creator, you might have a prospect with which to affect change. Marking mission accomplished.

Earlier this year (2012) I put my viral marketing theories to the test. With my friend and girlfriend I spent ~4 hours recording a funny parody video called "Sh*t Korean Girls Say." Random, I know.

I filmed the video for several reasons, but mostly

because I saw a huge explosion (aka "opportunity") on YouTube of videos with titles "Sh*t _____ _____ says." These included "white girls," "broke people," and many others that are too graphic for this book. Kidding. But don't get me wrong, I'm not suggesting viral marketing is a game of "fill in the blanks." What I am saying, however, is that there's always room for jumping on those "oops" moments we talked about earlier. Just do it.

After spending 4 hours capturing footage at 3-5 places around Atlanta and then spending another ~6 hours editing (I had no idea what I was doing), our finished product was ready to go around 4am.

To promote the video, my girlfriend and I did just one thing: we posted a link to the video along with a personalized call-to-action on ~100 friends' Facebook walls. In other words, I spammed 50 of my friends and she spammed 50 of her friends.

The result?

Within 24 hours we achieved 30,000+ views. This was from an initial outreach of only 100 people. The number is far from staggering, but it was a good exercise nonetheless.

Did our video go viral? Absolutely.

How do you know when content is viral? When it becomes [nearly] impossible to account for and trace all backlinks and referral traffic. Once that happens, your content has gone viral. There is no magic number or metric to measure otherwise.

Sounds exciting, right?! Now, let's break it down to see all the variables at play, specifically as they relate to my initial 5 trends of viral media.

1 | My video was super funny (in my opinion and a few thousand others')
2 | My video sparked a TON of conversation (controversial in nature, also topical and parodical)
3 | My video had concise, direct keyword phrases that mimicked other similarly themed videos. (Also, while I am a YouTube Partner, I didn't monetize this film until after 24 hours passed)
4 | My video was published in the midst of the explosion (again, "opportunity") of relevant videos with similar titles and themes
5 | My video didn't try to drive traffic to anything that would convert to my personal benefit, financial or otherwise

You see what we did there? We provided content that matched my 5 criteria (theories turned practicums) and experienced a modest taste of success. With all of this reinforcement, it might be time to give it another whirl. Or maybe you can.

By the way, to check out my video, go to pinff.com/korean.

The Power of Free
On that note, I think it's fitting to end this chapter on my favorite form of marketing: free samples.

A free sample can be a Microsoft Office 30-day trial, a cold can of Red Bull, or a free federal tax filing with Intuit's TurboTax. Whatever the case, free sells.

One of my favorite marketing lingo terms is "free 99." I got turned onto it by my friend Emily, who is a total catch and winner to say the least.

The idea is that since everything ends with a $.99 in the price point, so why not mock society and give stuff away with the same connotation?

From a consumer's standpoint (where I usually stand), I respect free because it implies transparency. It means the selling agent (company/cause/band/prostitute) isn't assuming you'll "take their word for it." That "word" is the marketing message, communicated through advertisements, press releases, and sales scripts. In doing so, the selling entity is also making them vulnerable to us, the consumer. And perhaps more importantly than all of that, a company that gives something away for free is humbling themselves by saying "Hi, I would really appreciate your business. Please give me a chance to satisfy your needs."

In today's society, that is an important connection to make. We already talked about our trendy hatred for "corporate," (rather, the "idea" of corporate) and the pressure that huge companies face to appear more personable or folksy than ever before. But free is a sacrifice, and free is humble. In translation, free means a huge deal to the consumer.

From a company's standpoint (where I sometimes stand), I am fascinated with free because it brings new meaning to the term "customer acquisition cost." See, companies spend money to get our business. A $1 million dollar ad might yield (indirectly, of course) an additional $5 million in sales revenues. Therefore it costs $5 per sale in ad expenses to acquire a customer. (Yes this is overly simplified, but just go with it.)

In the "free 99" world, however, a company is giving away a ton of *value* but at a fraction of the *cost*. Let me explain.

As I finish this book, Microsoft wants everybody to become interested in Windows 8, their latest operating system. The software will likely cost $100-200 per package, depending on the bells and whistles a user needs for their system.

Yet, at this moment, anyone can download a free BETA copy of Windows 8 with no obligation to purchase it later. Why?

Well, by giving away Windows 8 for a limited period of time, Microsoft is able to effectively afford the value of 100s of millions of dollars, while only paying the cost of the server space and maintenance to facilitate the downloads.

In addition to all the free trials and buzz that will inevitably follow, Microsoft also gets another benefit: customer feedback. Usually companies pay tons of money for "quality assurance surveys" (see: Taco Bell receipts), but Microsoft can get millions of pulse opinions and glitch reports for free. Beautiful, huh?

There's no doubt in my mind that free will continue to take over marketing metrics and create new avenues for rapid company growth. Free won't work in every industry, but for the average consumer, I predict that free marketing techniques will only become more prevalent in daily society. A catalyst to that change is the Daily Deal Phenomenon and, of course, our terrible economy.

As marketers, we have to envision the future and then spearhead the journey to that particular destination. As consumers, we have to protect ourselves and do what makes the most sense at the time.

Marketing may always get a bad rap. After all, people will always buy used cars. But if we understand it just a little bit better, we can sleep better at night knowing we are better informed than Steve Wozniak's father.

Suck it, engineers.

Why Marketing Matters

As mentioned at this chapter's opening, marketing comes in 100s of varietals, all with their own principles and famous people behind their formation. Which ones work best for your product will be different for every imaginable circumstance. What we covered here was not an expose of the best marketing tools, but an explanation of marketing as a whole, with a few in-depth conversations in between.

In case you're working on that next big thing, or just trying to be a more informed consumer, there are a few things to look out for, courtesy of this chapter's breakdown.

1 | Value benefits over features, and be skeptical of all things sales

2 | Appreciate good marketing messages, but always be sure to differentiate *needs* from *wants*

3 | Interpret numbers, trends, and consumer behaviors with a grain of salt. Make gut decisions, not statistically motivated ones.

4 | Be ambassadors of your favorite products. The more spotlight they receive, the better the service will be on your end.

5 | Don't be surprised when content, or a product, or a new way of thinking "takes off" into oblivion. Virality is among the purest by-products of the Information Age. Capitalize on it.

6 | Not everything is a gimmick. Perhaps "free" is the new "99 cents." Try it.

If you make a conscious decision to consider these 6 simple key learnings, you'll be a better marketer and consumer. You'll enhance the marketing machine, thus promoting higher quality output of its production. And that means better products, happier consumers, and a lot more *Gangnam Style* to go around.

Chapter 14 | Conclusions

A last bit of wordplay. Think of it as food for thought. At least that's why I eat before I write. Food for thought. Right?

Some of the initial themes and tones of this book changed after I decided to launch it on Kickstarter, which is an all-or-nothing funding platform for creative projects.

Here's how it works: a hopeful dreamer posts a project on the website, shares it with friends, and crosses fingers for financial gain. If the requested funding is pledged 100%, all pledgees are debited at the end of the campaign for their promised amount.

The premise behind Kickstarter is that the system makes things super easy and clean in case a project doesn't get funded, since no money exchanges hands until the end. This means no refunds, no disgruntled "investors," and most of all no additional stress beyond the general embarrassment of a failed funding campaign.

Since I was brand new to Kickstarter, I figured I would post a quick summary of my daily marketing activities before using it to raise funds for this book.

Through Kickstarter, I ultimately yielded $1,511 ($11 was the surplus) in 22 days. My approach was to make the budget tight enough to promote transparency while also loose enough to cover most every imaginable cost from production, shipping, ISBN registration, website hosting, copywriting, and editing.

To check out a comprehensive, staggered recount of my efforts to promote the pre-sales of this book, along with the costs associated (financial and time) and their perceived efficacy, head to pinff.com/presales. At the end of the post, I've written some notes on what I could have done better. The post will be updated accordingly after the book's release with more goodies, so be sure to check it out. My hope is that if you launch a project, you can learn from my mistakes (and successes!) and have an even more satisfying experience. If you just want to see my Kickstarter campaign page, go to pinff.com/kickstarter for the archived project.

(For another account of how I used popular social bookmarking site Reddit to achieve a huge spike in web traffic, read my case study at pinff.com/reddit.)

Moving on.

Never in my life did I believe it when writers say they have writer's block. I imagined they're all just latte-sipping anti-Americans with daddy issues. But after spending over $500 at coffee shops during the 2 years and 3 months it took me to write this book, let me tell you the "block" *does* exist.

I knocked out these last 10,000 words in just 7 days, a considerably disproportionate amount of progress given my daily average of ~50 words for 2 years. I attribute much of that success to my atmosphere, a secluded cabin in the north Georgia Mountains. In other words, I lived every writer's dream and it worked. It's amazing what we can accomplish if we put our mind to it.

All of it was courtesy of my good friend, Ty, who rented the cabin for his birthday week away from the city. Who would have thought I could eat, drink, and be merry, all while staying productive? Guess I have a little bit of credibility for converting desires into pursuit, like we learned about in Chapter 6 (Magnifying Glass).

Moving on.

I'm not a writer. I don't intend to be one and I have mad respect for those who are insanely more qualified than me to express themselves with the pen. But I am a life-long student. And to learn, we must do.

Timing is a strange creature. I recently found a notecard in my nightstand drawer that reads, "If you can't see the future, you aren't paying attention to the present." Maybe visionaries aren't so perceptive. Maybe they just understand what's right in front of their noses.

There's no telling where the next 5 years will take me—or you. But it's definitely taking us somewhere. We can embrace it and play our hand the best way we know how, or we can complain and ask the dealer for a new one. I don't suggest we live life like every day is our last. If that were the case, I would never have spent dozens of nights on Microsoft Word instead of watching reruns of *Cheers*. Not to mention you probably wouldn't be reading this, either.

People say money won't buy happiness. Maybe they're right. But a Wiki page will. I've put a lot of thought into what mine should look like, should I ever have one. To see it, head to pinff.com/wiki. Yeah, I'm totally a mess.

If you've made it this far, you have implicitly shown me more respect than I care to mention or compare with other people in my life. And for that, I thank you.

Now go outside, and be somebody.

##

Chapter 15 | Acknowledgements

The purpose of this final chapter is to thank the wonderful people who made this book possible.

Let's do that now.

First, to my lovely Kickstarter pledgees—you guys rock my world. I would not have had the strength to finish this project without the moral and financial support you all provided. As promised, here's a list of my Kickstarter supporters who were there for me long before these 35,000 words existed:

Sky Lee	Muneera Mak
Karen/Bob/Kevin Kulp	Bob Kulp Sr.
Kayla Cone	Bernadette Scruggs
Jonathan King	Greg Jarvis
Alex Dragu	Christine Shen
Eul Lee	Michael Peggs, Jr.
Kamilla Eliezer	Dacia Little
Andrew Freire	Kendra Kinnison
Bill Ehrlich	Daniel Kosmala
Aileen Cole	James Jin

Next, to my editor, who transformed incomplete thoughts and incoherent rants into rich, thought-provoking content that is entertaining, heart-felt, and meaningful. At least, I think so.

Jodie Blaney, you are a star.

(To hire her, visit pinff.com/Jodie)

And finally, to the authors, entrepreneurs, and lifestyle design bloggers who inspired me throughout college and in particular over the last 2 years to keep pushing, keep writing, and most importantly, keep learning.

S. Truett Cathy	C.S. Lewis
Jack Welch	Joshua Becker
Mark Cuban	Steve Jobs
Kamal Ravikant	Timothy Ferriss
Maneesh Sethi	Joshua Fields Millburn
Robert Kiyosaki	Seth Godin
Jason Fried	David Hansson
Michael E. Gerber	Glenn Beck

Props Where Props Are Due

For the most part, I used inline citations to give credit to researchers, surveys, opinion leaders, and other types of data that I don't take credit for creating myself. Below are some additional resources that further "back up" some of the more controversial data I presented for interpretation. If something you're looking to validate isn't included here, just use your super power Google skills to yield an answer. I always hated formatting, and this book may be my only chance to have it my way.

Enjoy.

http://www.intomobile.com/2012/02/29/apple-now-worth-well-over-500-billion-soon-become-wealthiest-company-ever/

http://www.forbes.com/sites/benzingainsights/2012/08/21/apple-now-most-valuable-company-in-history/

http://blogs.villagevoice.com/runninscared/2011/07/flip_flops_summer_wardrobe.php

http://www.cbsnews.com/2100-3445_162-2015684.html (ads daily, Chapter 13)

http://www.fa-mag.com/component/content/article/687.html?issue=32&magazineID=1&Itemid=27 (quote from *The Millionaire Next Door* about 80% of wealth being first generation)

http://bleacherreport.com/articles/1054264-super-bowl-advertisements-cost-per-viewer-well-worth-price-tag-for-companies (Super Bowl viewers / impressions)

http://magazine.nd.edu/news/1311/ (cheapest warehouse space in America, Ch. 8)

TMZ Staff (March 12, 2011). "Charlie Sheen Tour – Sold out in 18 minutes!". TMZ. Retrieved March 15, 2011. (Chapter 9)

http://www.census.gov/newsroom/releases/archives/families_households/cb10-174.html (average household size of America, Chapter 10)

http://behindthewall.nbcnews.com/_news/2012/08/24/13438436-as-she-nears-death-woman-who-saved-30-babies-from-trash-is-hailed-in-china?lite (story of woman in China who found 30 babies in trash cans, Chapter 10)

http://www.gatesfoundation.org/about/Pages/foundation-fact-sheet.aspx (Chapter 12, on new leaders giving money and Gates Foundation expending $25 billion)

Kane, Margaret (July 8, 2002). "eBay picks up PayPal for $1.5 billion." CNET News.com (CNET Networks). Retrieved 2007-11-13. (Chapter 8, on PayPal not yet being popular enough for potential use with WebVan)

http://smallbusiness.chron.com/profit-margin-supermarket-22467.html (Chapter 8, on WebVan having to start a grocery chain despite low profit margin)

Reference Guide – Short Links

Below is a recap of all short links provided in the book. Use this page as a reference for supplemental reading material so that you don't have to skim through a dozen pages for one link. I've also compiled these links at pinff.com/resources.

Pinff.com/brand (chapter 7, 4th dimension of brand, links to brand gap presentation)

Pinff.com/britney (Chapter 9, links to "Leave Britney Alone" YouTube video)

Pinff.com/cube (Chapter 7, links to *Cube* movie wiki page)

Pinff.com/gluco (Chapter 5, links to glucomannan supplement on Amazon)

Pinff.com/jodie (Chapter 15, links to my editor's personal website)

Pinff.com/karmin (Chapter 13, links to viral Karmin video on YouTube) Pinff.com/kickstarter (Links to archived web page of my Kickstarter funding campaign)

Pinff.com/korean (Chapter 13, links to "Sh*t Korean girls Sa"y YouTube video)

Pinff.com/linkedin (chapter 2, redirects to my LinkedIn profile)

Pinff.com/love (Chapter 5, links to "Love Yourself Like Your Life Depends On It" eBook)

Pinff.com/minimalism (Chapter 7, links to detailed testimony of my minimalist journey, along with a list of books and blogs to inspire your new favorite lifestyle)

Pinff.com/okgo (Chapter 13, links to OK GO YouTube videos that showcase subliminal advertising)

Pinff.com/personality (Chapter 7, redirects to famous Myers-Briggs personality test)

Pinff.com/presales (Chapter 14, links to journal of Kickstarter campaign)

Pinff.com/reddit (A case study blog post on how I used Reddit to boost web traffic)

Pinff.com/revolution (Chapter 13, links to Social Media Revolution YouTube video)

Pinff.com/song (Links to "All About You" music video, which got me a meeting with Sony HQ in NYC)

Pinff.com/travel (Links to travel hacking article by Maneesh Sethi)

Pinff.com/wiki (Ridiculous blog post outlining my dream Wiki page entry)

Finally, I thank my girlfriend, Sky, for her never-ending support of everything I am and aspire to be.

You are the reason I try.